Achieve Personal Growth

TIME
LIFE
BOOKS

MINDPOWER
JOURNEY THROUGH THE MIND AND BODY
COOKERY AROUND THE WORLD
LOST CIVILIZATIONS
THE ILLUSTRATED LIBRARY OF THE EARTH
SYSTEM EARTH
LIBRARY OF CURIOUS AND UNUSUAL FACTS
BUILDING BLOCKS
A CHILD'S FIRST LIBRARY OF LEARNING
VOYAGE THROUGH THE UNIVERSE
THE THIRD REICH
MYSTERIES OF THE UNKNOWN
TIME-LIFE HISTORY OF THE WORLD
FITNESS, HEALTH & NUTRITION
HEALTHY HOME COOKING
UNDERSTANDING COMPUTERS
THE ENCHANTED WORLD
LIBRARY OF NATIONS
PLANET EARTH
THE GOOD COOK
THE WORLD'S WILD PLACES

CONTENTS

INTRODUCTION

YOU HAVE IMMENSE POTENTIAL for personal growth, but if you're standing at the threshold of change, you might be confused about how to achieve greater confidence, self-awareness, and maturity. Perhaps you're feeling frustrated or "stuck" in life, or are trapped in a tough situation that, despite your best efforts, remains insoluble. There may be only one problematic area of your life, such as an unhappy relationship with someone in your family or an unreasonable employer, but if you cannot resolve an isolated but persistent problem, it can easily "leak" to another area of your life; your job, for example, might make you irritable or unapproachable at home, or so undermine your confidence that you withdraw from others. But if you're really stuck, every area of your life begins to feel like a prison, you may find yourself daydreaming about running away, and real growth becomes even harder. Is there any way out?

What's your attitude to change?

We all cling to what is familiar. When things are going reasonably well, it's all too easy to imagine that anything different means things will get worse, so we try not to rock the boat.

But what about changing for the better? Isn't it something we look forward to? The answer is, not necessarily. Facing *any* change of circumstances can be daunting because it means you have to move beyond what is familiar. Real growth demands genuine commitment, which is sometimes difficult to sustain over a long period of time. Do you have a pattern of hopeful, bright ideas followed by disappointment and lethargy? Everyone who has experienced a setback knows what this feels like, so you're not alone, but perhaps you need to consider the possibility that you might be trapped by your own beliefs or unconscious expectations that you don't deserve to be happy.

Start by defining goals

Children don't have goals—they just "do" whatever takes their fancy at the moment, and only as they get older do they begin to understand the concept of rewards. This realization then motivates them to "try" to be rewarded, and they begin to establish goals. They begin, that is, to think not only about what they want, but *how to get it*. Children learn, for example, that if they are sweet and obedient, or say "please" and "thank you," it's much more likely that a parent can be persuaded to be indulgent: buy them a special toy, let them stay an hour longer at a friend's house, or go on a school trip.

Although this shift in attitude sounds simple, in fact many adults find it difficult. They may also struggle to establish clear goals: specific outcomes that will enhance their lives and allow their individuality to flourish. Daydreaming about a new life might be a clue to your hopes and aspirations, but devising a step-by-step plan is an invaluable tool for getting yourself out of a rut.

Aim true

Perhaps the best way to get motivated is to look for inspiration to someone you think has grown in ways that you respect and admire—an effective technique known as "modeling." No matter what your intended activity or arena for growth is—work, relationships, or personal expression—it's very helpful to bear in mind that many successful people have probably known failure even if they don't admit it; eventually, they achieved their aims because they have four important qualities:

1. They are usually clear-sighted, and can remain focused on their desired goal.

2. Although they are single-minded about their goal, they are flexible about the means to attain it, and will try out different strategies.

3. They have the capacity to sacrifice short-term satisfaction for a long-term goal; they give something up in order to get what they want.

4. They are emotionally resilient, and whatever blow to their self-esteem or whatever setback they face, they have the confidence to believe that they can learn from their mistakes.

As well as modeling yourself on someone else, however, you have to be honest with yourself. *Achieve Personal Growth* will help you discover what *you* want, and will help you devise strategies for attaining better relationships, fulfilling work, and the most valuable—but perhaps most elusive—goal of all: self-acceptance and the courage to be all you are capable of being.

Time for transformation
*Once you have opened your eyes
to your own potential for growth
and glimpsed how much more life
could offer, you will want to take
risks and make changes to soar into
a whole new world of possibilities.*

WHAT IS GROWTH?

UNDERLYING MOST OF YOUR BEHAVIOR are assumptions about how the world works, or beliefs about "right" or "wrong." For example, you assume that your train will run reasonably on time, and when it doesn't, it upsets you; the lesson you learn is that an assumption might hold good most of the time, but not on *every* occasion. Similarly, many beliefs that are thought to be absolutely true may be disproven in the future. Once, the world was believed to be flat, an assumption that discouraged people from going too near "the edge" of the known world; eventually, a brave voyage of discovery confirmed that the world was round, and so began the European settlement of the New World.

We also hold beliefs about human nature. One of the difficulties you may face before embarking on a voyage of personal growth is the feeling that you cannot sail in an unknown direction, thinking "you can't change human nature," or that you've "always" been the way you are. But is this true?

What is the goal of personal growth?

Most of us in Western societies think of growth as the development of the individual marked by learning to understand and control behavior and emotions—fear, anger, love, or grief. By contrast, the Maori culture of New Zealand believes that the gods visit the person and cause these emotions, so it is not part of their culture to think that such emotions can be changed or developed.

The most significant difference between these two perspectives is that most of us are encouraged to believe that we are responsible for our own personal happiness, and can thus take steps to change our lives. One important way we can begin to grow and change is to uncover the hidden feelings that compel us to act in ways that may not contribute to our happiness. Sigmund Freud, the founding father of psychoanalysis, believed that if these repressed feelings could be brought out into the open, and the conscious mind could "see" them, we would have greater power to control our behavior, and to make

STRETCH YOURSELF

Are you bored by what is familiar, or stuck in your "comfort zone"? Do you think you could change with a little more inspiration and effort?

You probably can if you aim to go beyond what is familiar: trying new experiences, tackling new challenges, pushing yourself to learn and do more. How does this aid personal development? Stretching yourself enables you to:
• Broaden your horizons
• Learn new skills
• Develop your talents and qualities
• Build your confidence
• Pursue your goals
• Increase your self-esteem
• Achieve self-fulfillment.

An unexpected benefit is that, once you stretch in one area—work, for example—you'll have more confidence to stretch in other areas. You don't have to take huge risks: Start gradually, pushing yourself

gently in areas that make you anxious. If you're embarrassed about being clumsy, a "stretch" might involve joining a dance class; if you're shy, asking someone for a date would be a good challenge; if you always say yes to everyone, try saying no once in a while. You'll soon find that you instinctively know the areas you should tackle.

Do it gradually

You might try to "stretch" once a week, perhaps making it a joint effort with a friend; you could define your goals, and then check back with each other afterward to compare notes. To start with, you might try any of the following:
• Sign up for an evening class to learn a new language or skill, such as cooking or sculpture.
• Plan a weekend away in a new area. If you always do things with other people, consider going alone.
• Read a book different from the sort you would normally choose.

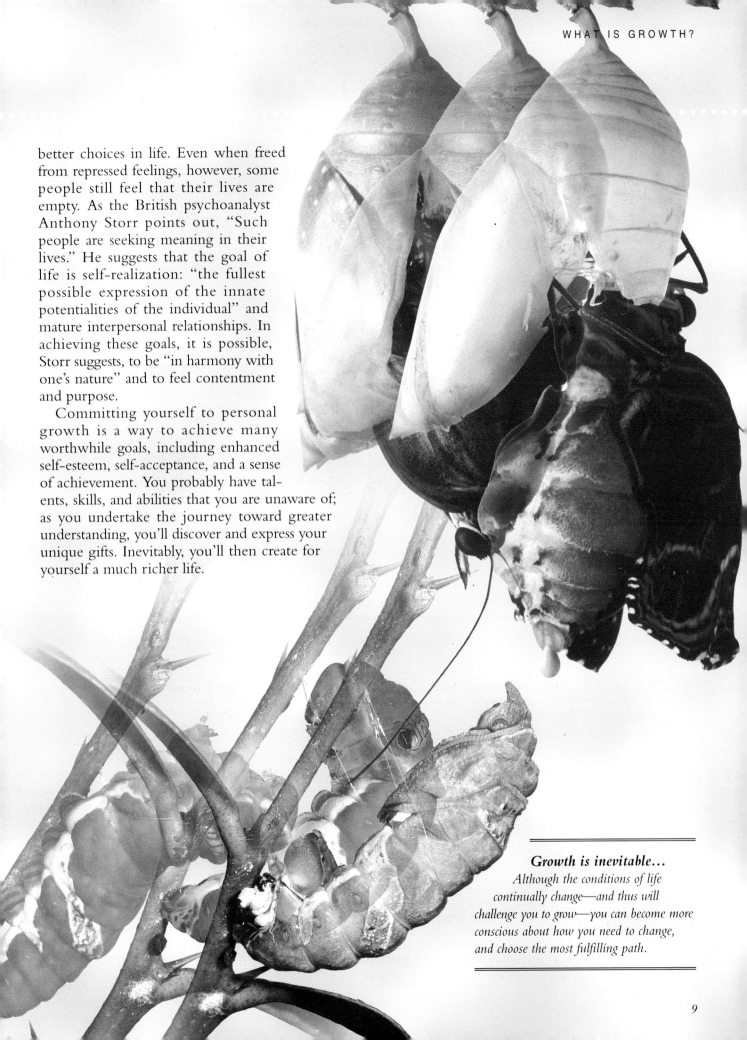

better choices in life. Even when freed from repressed feelings, however, some people still feel that their lives are empty. As the British psychoanalyst Anthony Storr points out, "Such people are seeking meaning in their lives." He suggests that the goal of life is self-realization: "the fullest possible expression of the innate potentialities of the individual" and mature interpersonal relationships. In achieving these goals, it is possible, Storr suggests, to be "in harmony with one's nature" and to feel contentment and purpose.

Committing yourself to personal growth is a way to achieve many worthwhile goals, including enhanced self-esteem, self-acceptance, and a sense of achievement. You probably have talents, skills, and abilities that you are unaware of; as you undertake the journey toward greater understanding, you'll discover and express your unique gifts. Inevitably, you'll then create for yourself a much richer life.

Growth is inevitable...
Although the conditions of life continually change—and thus will challenge you to grow—you can become more conscious about how you need to change, and choose the most fulfilling path.

FOCUSING ON GROWTH

Taking your first steps on the path of personal growth is easier if you can identify which areas of your life you want to concentrate on most. Perhaps you're basically content, but want to tap your creativity; or you may know that you want to make changes in your work life, but don't know how to make them. Read all the questions on this and the next page, jotting down relevant pages; this simple self-assessment exercise will help you focus your energies and begin the greatest journey of your life.

1. Are you basically happy?

YES: Even if you're content, you might find you need a little excitement or something new in your life. See "Where Do I Go From Here?" pp. 134-135.

NO: In which area(s) are you most frustrated?
• Your inner self?
See Questions 3 and 5
• Your intimate relationships?
See Question 9
• Your family relationships?
See Question 10
• Your work life?
See Questions 11 and 12
• Your creativity?
See Question 3
• Your spirituality?
See Questions 5 and 13

Free to grow
Some areas of your life may flourish more than others because your confidence is more deeply rooted.

2. Do you know what you want in life?

YES: Although it's important to know what you want, you may become stressed if you try to control everything; if you have a rigid outlook, your inflexibility might make it harder to cope with disappointment. Try to remain open to new opportunities—and let yourself be spontaneous! See "Give Chance a Chance," pp. 58-59.

NO: Before you can achieve goals, you need to focus on what would suit you, what your strengths are, and especially what you believe about yourself. See "Who Are You?" pp. 34-35, and "Get in Touch," pp. 38-39.

3. Do you enjoy time by yourself?

YES: You probably pursue some form of creative expression. If you want to take this further, see "Tap Your Talents," pp. 52-53.

NO: Being comfortable in your own company is a sign of self-acceptance. It might help if you set time aside for solitude to discover the quieter, more reflective side of yourself. See "Find a Quiet Place," pp. 126-127 and "But I Can't Draw!" pp. 54-55.

6. Do you want to move forward?

YES: Most people have greater strength and more talent and skills than they use. You can probably achieve whatever you set your mind on. See "What's Stopping You?" pp. 88-89.

NO: You may want to focus on inner growth instead. If you're interested in developing the more introspective or creative side of your personality, see "But I Can't Draw!" pp. 54-55 and "Courses and Retreats," pp. 130-131.

4. Do you have faith in your ability to make changes?

YES: You are probably an optimist, and enjoy stretching yourself. Most likely you've coped successfully with problems in the past, and try to learn from your mistakes. To keep growing, see "Create a Challenge," pp. 120-121.

NO: Perhaps you lack confidence or have yet to resolve inner conflicts— or perhaps you haven't discovered what you're good at. See "Change Your Thinking," pp. 30-31, "What's Stopping You?" pp. 88-89, "Self-Defeating Behavior," pp. 110-111, and "Take a Leap of Faith," pp. 122-123.

7. Are you glad to be you?

YES: Self-esteem is the bedrock of happiness and growth. You're on the right track. See the next two pages.

NO: Discontent can be a great spur to growth, and provide the motivation you need to change what you don't like about yourself or a particular life situation. See "Change Your Thinking," pp. 30-31, "Self-Defeating Behavior," pp. 110-111, "Discover Your Real Needs," pp. 36-37, and "You Are What You Are," pp. 82-83.

5. Do you feel contentment and a sense of inner peace?

YES: Even though you have inner serenity, remember that growth never stops, so continue to expand your horizons and develop your awareness. See "Create a Challenge," pp. 120-121, and "Where Do I Go From Here?" pp. 134-135.

NO: Do you feel bored and frustrated, and do you need to be stimulated by diversions that make it hard to commit yourself to anything? Are you rushing around in an attempt to hide painful feelings? See "Addicted to Action," pp. 100-101.

HEAD FOR THE SUN

8. Do you find your relationships rewarding?

YES: You may still find that your creativity and inner life need time and attention. See "Enhance Your Imagination," pp. 48-49, and "Find a Quiet Place," pp. 126-127.

NO: You probably feel lonely, and your difficulties may be rooted in lessons learned from your family. Also, if you try to grow, you may be frustrated by the expectations of others. See "The Growing Family," pp. 68-69, "Growing Together," pp. 72-73, and "Telling Others," pp. 116-117.

9. Do your intimate relationships allow you to grow?

YES: You've probably learned how to assert yourself without alienating partners or friends. Now that you have "space" to grow, you might want to explore things on your own. See "Find a Quiet Place," pp. 126-127, and "Where Do I Go From Here?" pp. 134-135.

NO: All of us struggle with the fear of revealing our innermost thoughts and emotions, but it's important to be true to yourself and to explain to others how and why you want to change. See "Private Self, Public Self," pp. 70-71, "Growing Together," pp. 72-73, "The Ripple Effect," pp. 106-107, and "Telling Others," pp. 116-117.

10. Do you have a good relationship with your parents and siblings?

YES: Having good family relationships is an important source of our self-esteem, helping us to develop confidence so that we live life to the full, and supporting us when things don't work out as we expected. You're on track to achieving a balance between your inner and outer worlds. See "Making Connections," pp. 64-65.

NO: Perhaps you were taught that you had no right to be yourself or to have independent goals and dreams. It's never too late to change limiting behavior patterns. See "The Growing Family," pp. 68-69.

11. Do you find your work fulfilling?

YES: Is there a danger that you define yourself only through work? See "You Are What You Are," pp. 82-83. If you're not sure what work means to you, see "Just the Job?" pp. 78-79.

NO: Doing work that you enjoy or believe in provides most of us with an important source of meaning and purpose. If you're stuck or frustrated, see "Is Your Career on Course?" pp. 80-81.

12. Have you achieved success in your work?

YES: Well done! But if you feel you still have more to offer, see "Successful and Stuck?" pp. 84-85.

NO: To discover which obstacles are preventing you from achieving success, see "What's Stopping You?" pp. 88-89, "Fear of Failure," pp. 92-93, and "Fear of Success," pp. 94-95.

13. Do you know how to find greater fulfillment in life?

YES: You seem to have achieved a balance in your life, but perhaps you need a new challenge. See "Where Do I Go from Here?" pp. 134-135.

NO: It might be worthwhile to seek out new sources of growth. You probably have a great deal of untapped talent and energy that you can harness to help you grow. See "Courses and Retreats," pp. 130-131.

CHAPTER ONE

YOUR GROWTH POTENTIAL

EACH OF US has enormous potential for personal growth, and, to some degree, we change and develop naturally—learning from our experiences, handling setbacks with greater wisdom and maturity, and revising our attitudes, priorities, and expectations. We can also choose to be active directors of this process, however. We can decide to make full use of our potential in every area of our lives, so that we become happier and feel more fulfilled and alive.

As we move from infancy to childhood, through puberty to adulthood, our physical growth is paralleled by psychological and emotional growth. "Facts of Life," pages 16-17, looks at the importance of turning points in our lives and at how we sometimes have to let go of aspects of our old selves in order to move forward and embrace new opportunities and priorities.

We all have secret dreams, but unless we commit ourselves to striving for what we really want, they remain as no more than dreams. "Desires into Goals," pages 20-21, describes how to focus your energies and efforts on specific targets, and how to devise a realistic plan with a succession of achievable goals in order to make your dreams come true.

The biggest factor influencing your potential for growth is your attitude. The questionnaire "What's Your Attitude?" on pages 22-25 will help you identify specific areas of your life, such as work or personal relationships, where you might want to make changes. You can use the qualities, skills, and inner resources you find effective in one area to help you get the results you want in another.

No matter what your intended change is—moving house, retraining for a new career, getting fit, or freeing yourself from limiting attitudes and ways of behaving—you need clarity and a strong inner conviction to carry you through. Identifying your priorities, rather than trying to overhaul your life in one go, helps to ensure that your changes are the right ones for you, and that you take them at a manageable pace (see "Do You Want to Change?" pp. 26-27).

A great measure of your capacity for growth is your ability to move on from problems. A setback need never be a failure if you learn from it and use it to your advantage. "Change Your Focus," pages 28-29, explores how setbacks can guide you on a new path, while "Change Your Thinking," pages 30-31, emphasizes the importance of believing in yourself.

SIMPLY OPENING UP YOUR MIND TO THE POSSIBILITY OF GROWTH

WILL GIVE YOU A GLIMPSE OF THE IMMENSE POTENTIAL

YOU HAVE WITHIN YOU.

FACTS OF LIFE

THE ANCIENT GREEK philosopher Heraclitus, who observed that everything in the universe is in a perpetual state of flux, wrote that, "Nothing endures but change." The cycle of birth and death is an inescapable reality that governs everything: Night follows day, winter gives way to spring, a seed grows into a plant and then dies, and a rock is pummeled by wind and sea into grains of sand. Change—perceived as growth, development, maturity, and gradual fading away—is the dynamic law of life.

The life cycle

For all living creatures, physical growth starts from the moment of conception and continues until full maturity has been reached. In human beings, this physical growth is accompanied by a continuous and lifelong process of mental and emotional growth, from which we develop a sense of self. Nature provides us with a "development clock," signifying when one stage of development ends and another begins. For example, babies become more independent from their mothers because certain activities, such as the ability to walk or feed themselves, are "natural" developments (although they can be encouraged). As children get older, they form new attachments outside the family, and each new relationship is a new chapter in their personal development and evolving maturity.

Rehearsing for life

A teacher who encourages his or her young pupils to pretend to be a seed that grows into a flower or tree is helping them to learn that growth involves change.

Turning points

Ideally, each successive stage from babyhood to old age heralds another step along the road to becoming a wiser, more fulfilled person. Our journey takes us from being a child through adolescence to adulthood, from exploration and learning to an active working life, and finally into retirement.

Very often, we celebrate the successful completion of certain tasks or expectations, such as when we have a party upon graduation or retirement. Other turning points, such as marriage, guide us toward responsibilities: They are occasions for joy, but also alert us to the fact that new challenges lie ahead. Such milestones are important because they provide an opportunity to participate consciously in our own development. We recognize that we are on the threshold of new growth.

For this reason, milestones can feel daunting. Birthdays, for example, may bring home the stark reality of time passing. For both men and women, their thirtieth birthday can be quite traumatic, a reminder that no-one is young forever. For some, however, it is a welcome end to the period that Gail Sheehy, author of *Passages*, describes as the "trying twenties," and at its best, the next decade can be a time of new vitality and of renewed commitment to new or more realistic goals.

When to let go

Growth encompasses both danger and opportunity. It might bring you moments of crisis because it forces you to re-examine your identity or the direction you're taking, and you will inevitably ask yourself many questions, such as, "Why am I doing all this? Do I really want to change? What do I really believe in? What do I really want?"

Growth also requires that you *let go* or give something up, and this can be hard. We often think of growth in terms of having more of something—more happiness, more money, more recognition—but there are times when *less* is liberating and serves personal growth better. You may need more time to pursue a private dream, but first may need to let go of time-wasting diversions. You should expect to feel grief for those aspects of your old self that must be left behind. The compensation will be that, once you commit yourself to growth and renewal, you can build a fuller and happier life—and an identity that is yours and yours alone.

Marking your path

Birthdays and other milestones—such as graduation, marriage, or retirement—are often celebrated to mark their significance. Each stage of life is a distinctive phase of growth.

GROWING PAINS

We spend the first half of our lives building foundations: getting an education, creating goals, finding out what we're best suited for, and perhaps getting married and starting a family. In the second half of our lives, however, our task seems to focus on shoring up those same foundations and coping with loss, as our relationships change, our children leave home, family or friends become ill or die, and we retire from a lifetime of work. While these are losses we should expect to encounter, life is unpredictable, and crises can occur at any time.

Change can be painful

Suffering is part and parcel of life, and is a reality that no-one can escape. Hopes are dashed, ideals are tarnished, cherished dreams crumble, and sooner or later loved ones die. But it is also true that suffering—possibly more than joy—has much to teach us. Suffering strips us of our protective layer, connects us to our deeper selves—what we really believe in, our true strengths and weaknesses—and forces us to question the very nature of our existence. Indeed, for some, it is the experience of suffering that first awakens their desire for self-discovery and growth; people realize that their view of themselves and the world may be distorted. When life challenges our ideas or interpretation, development and change—even when unsought— inevitably occur.

Tending your inner garden

You may not think that you're well equipped to cope with a crisis, but you probably have gifts that are uniquely yours and deserve to be nurtured. Disappointment and sorrow are part of living and, as such, have much to contribute to your understanding of life and your place in it. This is not to say that wisdom is exclusively gained by adversity, but by accepting the reality of loss, you can redefine yourself and support your future growth.

Elizabeth, for example, had always been reflective and self-aware, and while bringing up four children, had always made time for reading, listening to music, and solitary country walks. When her husband died at the early age of 47, her shock and grief were acute. In an effort to come to terms with her loss, she began writing poetry. "It was a genuine outpouring of the heart," she told a close friend,

"It was as though I found a voice for both my pain and my joy, and I could express thoughts and feelings I couldn't articulate in any other way." The six months she wrote compulsively were, for her, six months of profound creative and spiritual growth.

Believe in yourself

What you expect from life is very often what you get. If you believe that only the young deserve to feel hopeful and positive, then the evidence of your later years will probably confirm this preconception. If, on the other hand, you have faith in your capacity to mature, broaden, and diversify your interests, then there is little doubt that, no matter what your age, you will continue to create new opportunities to find joy in life. Even when you face difficulties, if you believe you can find the strength to cope—perhaps by turning to others for sympathy and support—it's far more likely that you will overcome life's many challenges, and emerge a stronger, more fulfilled person as a result.

Limitless horizons
An affirmative belief is like a doorway opening onto a garden of untold opportunity. Believing in your capacity to grow will make it easier to take a risk, or to cope when life takes an unexpected turn.

A CREATIVE LIFE

Most people would recognize the name Beethoven, if not the composer's music. Although he gave recitals from the age of seven, his true genius, which was for composing, did not mature until much later in his life; indeed, his early compositions were regarded only as clever—not brilliant—exercises. His story is not one of easy, progressive growth and development. Throughout his life, he also had to contend with profound disappointments: ill health, sorrowful love affairs, and, most tragically, gradual hearing loss from the age of 31 that ultimately left him completely deaf.

Despite the drawbacks of living in a silent world, Beethoven's awesome spiritual and creative powers continued to grow. In fact, the years during which his hearing declined were marked by prolific creativity.

Of Beethoven's Ninth Symphony, completed when he was 54, the great German composer Richard Wagner said it was "the landmark of an entirely new period in the history of universal art."

Enduring creativity

The fact that Beethoven's rich creative life continued to flourish in the face of hardship and physical disability is an enduring source of inspiration to anyone who may need to re-create a sense of purpose in life after suffering disappointment. It serves as a reminder that, in many ways, growth can be enhanced, rather than eroded, by profound loss.

DESIRES INTO GOALS

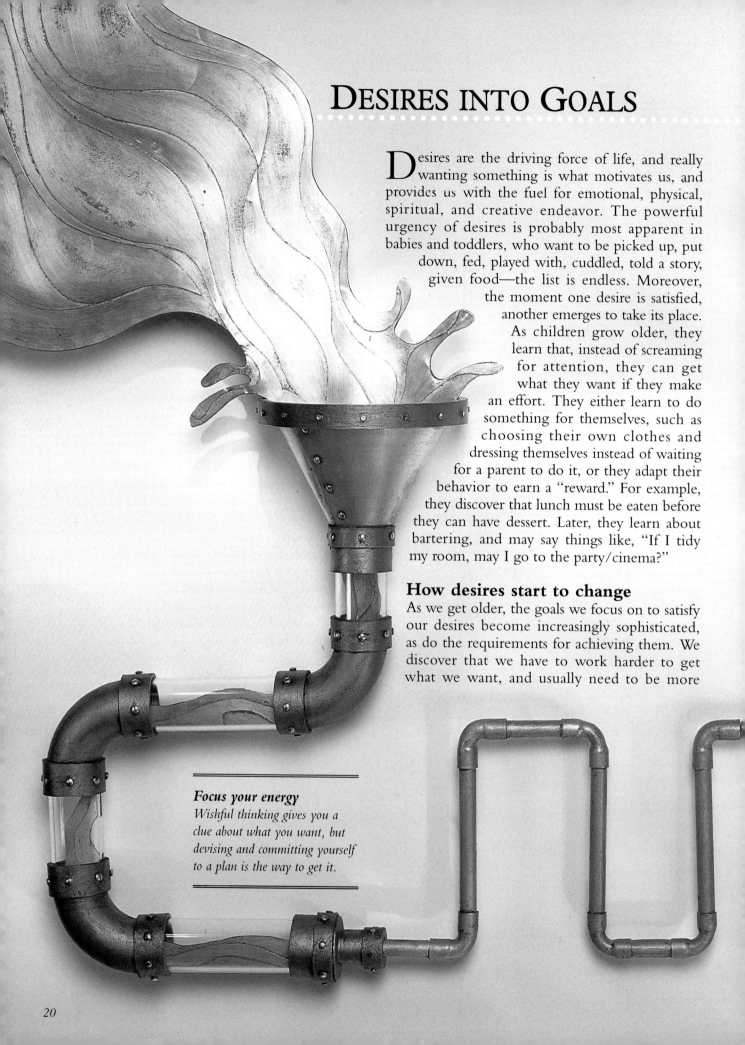

Desires are the driving force of life, and really wanting something is what motivates us, and provides us with the fuel for emotional, physical, spiritual, and creative endeavor. The powerful urgency of desires is probably most apparent in babies and toddlers, who want to be picked up, put down, fed, played with, cuddled, told a story, given food—the list is endless. Moreover, the moment one desire is satisfied, another emerges to take its place.

As children grow older, they learn that, instead of screaming for attention, they can get what they want if they make an effort. They either learn to do something for themselves, such as choosing their own clothes and dressing themselves instead of waiting for a parent to do it, or they adapt their behavior to earn a "reward." For example, they discover that lunch must be eaten before they can have dessert. Later, they learn about bartering, and may say things like, "If I tidy my room, may I go to the party/cinema?"

How desires start to change

As we get older, the goals we focus on to satisfy our desires become increasingly sophisticated, as do the requirements for achieving them. We discover that we have to work harder to get what we want, and usually need to be more

Focus your energy
Wishful thinking gives you a clue about what you want, but devising and committing yourself to a plan is the way to get it.

BE REALISTIC

While some people avoid setting any goals, others spend their lives reaching for the moon but never getting there. With reckless abandon, they chase after impossible dreams only to be left bruised, battered, and frustrated when they fail to realize them. How can you prevent this from happening to you?

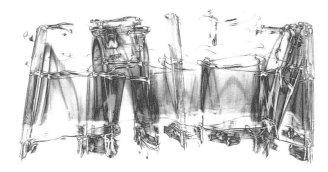

Taking the first step

Everyone needs a vision or dream to feel inspired, but many of us need to learn how to get going. While it's important to stretch yourself, keep your "big dream" within reach by approaching it slowly but surely. The easiest and most effective thing you can do is to set yourself a succession of modest goals and write them down; then, as you tick or cross off each goal as you accomplish it, you can enjoy a sense of achievement and personal fulfillment. Your confidence will grow—and the next step will be that much easier. Compare yourself to a writer who, in order to become successful, needs to start with the very first word on a dauntingly blank page. Jottings that seem inconsequential at first may contain the seeds of a stimulating and cohesive idea.

determined in our efforts. Unfortunately, many people find adult life so daunting precisely because they *cannot* focus on what they want, or don't modify their behavior. They may give up the notion of having objectives and achieving them, and instead muddle along feeling powerless and dissatisfied—never forging their own path, but simply resigning themselves to what they see as "fate."

Changing "I wish" to "I will"

A wish is based on a desire that you regard as being out of reach. A goal, on the other hand, is a specific outcome to which you intend to commit yourself, and for which you can devise a particular strategy.

If you shy away from the effort needed to change "I wish" to " I will," it may be because you're afraid of making the wrong choice or of being disappointed (see "Fear of Failure," pp. 92-93).

Colin, for example, wanted to return to college for a degree, but could not decide whether he wanted to study business or law. Because he has been stuck at the stage of wishful thinking for ten years, he now, at 35, is stuck doing unsatisfying work that he feels is beneath him, but is unable to change.

Nobody achieves every goal, of course. Even the goals you do achieve might not deliver the happiness or satisfaction you expected. Despite this, and despite the pain and disappointment a failure may engender, it is still important to commit yourself to your goals: They are what give momentum and direction to life—and are ultimately what keep you going and make life worthwhile.

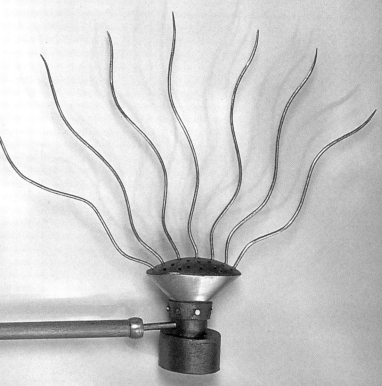

What's Your Attitude?

OWEVER EAGER and ready to embark on your own unique journey of personal growth you are, you may find it very difficult to make changes in certain areas. While your underlying attitudes and beliefs may facilitate growth in some directions, they may hinder you in others. This questionnaire is designed to help you determine what motivates you, and to what degree you are comfortable setting your own agenda for change. It should also help you identify areas of your life that might require more attention and commitment from you in order to change.

The questions are grouped into four different categories: Yourself, Personal Relationships, Work, and Friends and Community. For each statement, choose the answer **a**, **b**, or **c**, depending upon which response most closely matches your own. Then turn to page 138 for comments and an analysis of your results.

What are you hiding away?

You probably have many hidden talents that never see the light of day because certain attitudes or beliefs may be holding you back. Discovering these hidden beliefs, and pinpointing aspects of your life where you need to change, will help foster personal growth.

Yourself

1. You decide to set yourself the target of reading at least one book a week because:
 a) Other people always seem better read and able to discuss things more easily than you are.
b) It will give you more to talk about at parties.
c) You feel it would expand your mind.

2. You feel it is important to deepen your understanding of yourself because:
a) If you don't, other people will always tell you what to think or what you really want.
b) Personal growth is very fashionable.
c) Everything starts with self-knowledge.

3. You consider losing weight because:
a) Your partner made hurtful and disparaging remarks about your body.
b) Magazine articles suggest that thin people are more desirable and are more successful.
c) Being overweight has made you feel very unfit, and you want to be healthier.

4. Your best friend suggests joining an evening class in French. You agree because:
a) Your friend says that you should try to broaden your horizons.
b) You think speaking French will impress others.
c) You love French culture and have always wanted to speak the language.

5. You feel it is important to give up smoking because:
a) You're tired of your friends and family nagging you about how it undermines your health.
b) It's a habit that others regard as unintelligent and socially unacceptable.
c) You know that smoking can seriously damage your health, and you want to break a self-destructive habit.

Personal Relationships

1. You decide you want to become more sexually adventurous because:

a) You feel that your partner will be more interested in you and find you more exciting.

b) You feel that people are expected to experiment sexually these days, and to be unconventional.

c) You recognize that you're not entirely comfortable with your sexual feelings, and would like to express them more freely and to be less inhibited.

2. You want to try to be more open about your feelings because:

a) People have told you that you bottle everything up and should let go more.

b) Experts always stress the importance of communication and expressing yourself.

c) You feel that sharing feelings strengthens bonds of intimacy and understanding.

3. You decide to make a conscious effort to improve your relationship with your partner's aloof and critical mother because:

a) Your partner says that the animosity and tense atmosphere between you and his or her mother is upsetting, and makes family gatherings impossible.

b) You don't want to be seen as the person who is responsible for causing unhappiness, anger, or tension in the family.

c) You realize things must change and, whether or not you are to blame, you're prepared to review your attitude in order to start the ball rolling.

4. You resolve to try to spend more time and do more things together with your partner because:

a) He or she has complained more than once of feeling a bit lonely and neglected by you.

b) You feel that couples are expected to do things, share activities and interests, and spend lots of time together.

c) You realize that you haven't been giving your relationship much attention recently, and you want to strengthen your relationship and create greater intimacy by sharing new things.

5. You are accused of being too demanding and critical by your partner or by other friends. You want to do something about this because:

a) You worry that your partner may find you too difficult and leave you.

b) You are concerned about how your behavior may appear to others.

c) You acknowledge that it is a negative and unappealing trait, which, if left unchecked, could seriously damage your relationships.

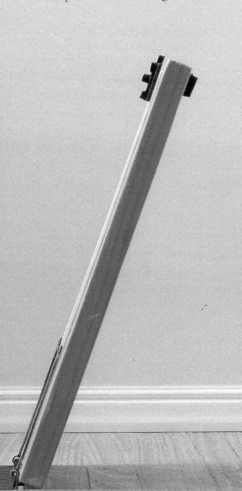
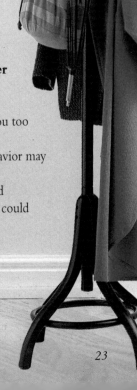

Work

1. You decide to ask your boss for a raise because:
a) Your colleagues persuade you that it's your right, even though you're unsure whether you deserve it.
b) You'd like to be seen as more dynamic and go-getting.
c) You're confident that you're doing a good job, and you want your efforts to be acknowledged and rewarded.

2. You decide to invest in taking a management course because:
a) Everyone has told you that you'll get nowhere without it.
b) A colleague did and got promoted.
c) You realize that there are skills you need to achieve your goals.

3. You resolve to change jobs because:
a) Your friends say you're not being valued.
b) You can't get on with your workmates.
c) You know your talents are being wasted and would be better employed in another capacity.

4. You submit a suggestion for increased efficiency because:
a) You've heard it's a good way to curry favor with the boss.
b) You want to impress your colleagues with your initiative and originality.
c) You are convinced the changes you suggest are necessary and will benefit everyone.

5. You decide to become more conscientious, competent, and productive at work because:
a) People have warned you that you may lose your job if you don't.
b) You keep getting reprimanded.
c) You realize your lack of commitment in the past has held you back, and you know you will feel greater self-esteem and fulfillment if you take pride in working well.

Friends and community

1. You decide to join a campaign to stop the closure of a local library because:
a) Even though you don't think it's an important issue, you feel pressured by the organizers to get involved.
b) You believe people would think you were selfish and not concerned about the community if you refused.
c) You feel that a library is a vital asset to the community.

2. You plan to start having dinner parties because:
a) You feel it is expected of you.
b) Everyone else seems to do it.
c) Although you feel nervous, you want to express to your friends how much you enjoy their company.

3. You decide to make a donation to a charity that one of your friends supports because:
a) Refusing his or her request for a contribution would make you feel very uncomfortable.
b) You feel it is important to do the right thing and that if your friend supports this charity, you should support it, too.
c) You decide that good intentions are not enough, and it's time you started putting your money where your mouth is.

4. Your oldest friend has split up with his or her partner and asks to come and stay with you for a few days. You agree because:
a) You find it impossible to refuse, even though you feel uncomfortable about it, and don't know what to say.
b) You feel that he or she would do the same for you.
c) It's important to offer your friend support during what you know is a very difficult, painful time.

5. Your neighbor calls with a leaflet about a new scheme for recycling domestic waste. You decide to participate because:
a) All your neighbors will be taking part.
b) You fear that you'll be seen to be irresponsible if you don't get involved.
c) You believe that everyone must play a part to safeguard the environment.

Use your resources

Once you have read the analysis of your responses to this questionnaire on page 138, consider the steps outlined below to help you make progress in the areas where you want to develop. These areas will offer you the greatest potential for transformation and growth, and give you the chance to use your toolbox of personal resources. Every problem is different, and often a specific approach or strategy is required to overcome it. The effort involved in overcoming shyness, for example, is different from the demands of trying to become more efficient in the way you use your time, or more understanding with your friends. One requirement applies to all areas, however: Be specific from the outset about what you want to achieve.

Steps to success

Whenever you set yourself goals, write them down to pledge your commitment seriously and help keep you on track. Seeing your goals on paper makes them more tangible and fixes them in your mind. There may be unforeseen occurrences, of course, which will necessitate your modifying your approach, or even starting afresh. Don't make your plans so rigid that you turn your back on unexpected opportunities for change. Your willingness and capacity to be flexible and take advantage of changing circumstances is one of the key factors for making your life the way you want it.

It is also helpful to formulate a step-by-step plan to structure your actions, and to ensure that each step complements and reinforces the previous one. If you want a more interesting job, for example, how can you improve your chances of getting one? Do you need to improve your skills? Are there extra qualifications that could help you? Does your appearance need smartening up? Whatever you want to change—whether it's decorating your house, learning new

skills, or forging new relationships or greater self-esteem—a sensible plan will help achieve your goal.

Finally, when considering the areas that currently cause you problems, remind yourself of the things you *can* do, and the qualities you already have. Positive traits are resources you can apply to many different situations. For example, if you demonstrate initiative and are creative at work, you could approach family problems with similar flexibility. If you are a sympathetic and understanding friend, try bringing this quality to bear when dealing with a prickly colleague at work. You could also harness these traits to be gentler and more compassionate toward yourself, which in turn will improve your self-esteem.

DO YOU WANT TO CHANGE?

BEHIND A SUCCESSFUL LIFE CHANGE is the determination to bring it about. Conscious change is a dynamic process and you can't afford to be halfhearted about it: You need to fix your objective clearly in your mind, then take action to move toward it. For example, Christopher was forever announcing his intention to sort out his finances and clear his debts. He didn't ever manage it, however, because he was unwilling to curtail his free-spending lifestyle, and he tended to blame rising costs rather than his own lack of resolve.

A similar problem can arise if the desire to change is the result of outside suggestion. Television and magazines are constantly promoting the idea that we should be sexier, more ambitious, more career-minded, more assertive, and so on. Friends and family may also offer advice on how we should change to become happier or more fulfilled. Janice's mother, for instance, frequently nagged her to be more sociable and gregarious, prodding her to go to

parties and join in girls' nights out with her colleagues. When Janice did go, however, she didn't enjoy herself; she found that she genuinely preferred spending time at home on her hobbies—making silver jewelry and playing the piano.

Change that is forced upon you, or that does not spring from an inner conviction, is unlikely to affect your life in a meaningful or lasting way. To ensure that your heart is truly committed to whatever change you are pursuing, listen to your inner voice; only then will you be fully focused and motivated to bring that change about.

Know your priorities

When contemplating your intended changes, you need to identify your priorities. All change can be stressful, so it is usually unwise to try to tackle everything at once. For example, Craig was dissatisfied with almost every aspect of his life: His job was boring and badly paid, his relationship with his

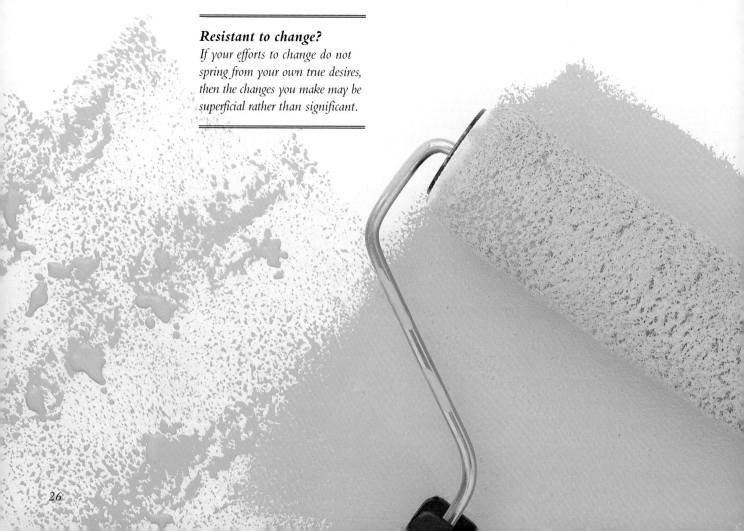

Resistant to change?
If your efforts to change do not spring from your own true desires, then the changes you make may be superficial rather than significant.

ADDICTED TO CHANGE

While some people view the prospect of change with fear and reluctance, others seem constantly to seek it out. The moment anything becomes settled and predictable, they feel compelled to turn life on its head and start again, addicted to the buzz of fresh challenges, new circumstances, and the idea of something better and more exciting just around the corner. They may, for example, become restless when a relationship changes from the first flush of intense romance to a steadier, everyday reality, or embark on a new home improvement project almost before the paint has dried on the last. Life is a chronicle of shifting directions and interests. It is change for change's sake, not because a new approach or idea is actually needed.

People like this are often driven by a constant sense of dissatisfaction; every dream quickly becomes tarnished, every hope easily soured by disillusionment. Because they don't commit themselves to seeing things through, and can't accept that most things require consistent application and spade work, the seeds they plant rarely have a chance to bear fruit.

All change
Constantly turning your life upside down can make you feel busy and active, but you may not feel contented or fulfilled, or that you are achieving what you really want in life.

girlfriend seemed to be going nowhere, he was physically unfit, and he hated sharing an apartment with his brother. He felt things either had to change or he would go mad. In the space of one week, he quit his job, broke up with his girlfriend, and ended up sleeping on a friend's sofa after a huge argument with his brother. Not surprisingly, this plunged him into emotional and practical chaos. Instead of making changes in a considered and constructive way, he landed himself with a new set of problems that made him feel just as trapped and ineffectual as before.

Plan ahead

If change is to be effective and beneficial, you need to think it through clearly in advance so that you understand its implications. In Craig's case, the discontent he felt in his job partly contributed to the problems he was having with his girlfriend and brother. His anger and frustration built up during the day, and then invariably spilled over into his private life when he got home. If he had addressed the job situation first—perhaps by taking a training course to acquire new skills—he would have been in a better position to evaluate the other changes he wanted to make.

In general, you are likely to give priority to the changes you feel are most important, or to the areas currently causing you anguish or frustration. There are times, however, when it is better to start with changes that are smaller or easier to make. Indra, for example, felt exactly the way Craig did, and that her whole life needed an overhaul: She wanted to leave her job in marketing and retrain as a teacher, resolve a long-standing disagreement with her sister, learn to swim, and move to a larger apartment. While recuperating from a bout of flu that left her feeling exhausted, she decided to draw up a list. Wisely, however, she realized that she didn't have the emotional or physical energy to initiate the weightier changes, so she decided that she would first recharge her batteries by switching to a more nutritious diet and exercising regularly. Once she had achieved these changes, she felt ready to tackle the first step on her list.

CHANGE YOUR FOCUS

The key to personal growth is the capacity to change. We develop when we initiate changes effectively, or when we respond to changes brought about by circumstances, other people, or the inevitable transitions of life. We cannot stop the onset of puberty, being disappointed in love, suffering setbacks, ageing, and so on. We can, however, work at having an attitude that equips us to view change optimistically and with an open mind, and to make the most of the opportunities it brings.

Update your agenda

The fact that nothing is carved in stone is something that inspires hope as well as regret, for while we might wish to freeze-frame moments of happiness or triumph in our minds forever, we are equally eager to move on from pain or adversity. For every person who says, "Wouldn't it be wonderful if things could always stay like this?" there is someone else thinking, "I can't wait for all this to be over."

When you were 15, your principal aims may well have been escaping from parental control and enjoying yourself. A few years later, your priorities probably included getting a job and finding a suitable boy- or girlfriend. Each stage of life is accompanied by a new set of practical and psychological demands, hopes, and aspirations. Sometimes we respond to the new challenges with optimism and gusto. At other times, updating our agenda is an uphill struggle.

Joanna, for instance, devoted ten years to being a wife and mother. She derived great satisfaction from this role, and when her youngest child started school, Joanna felt lonely and directionless. From being a cheerful, easygoing person, she became irritable and depressed. Her response to her children's growing independence was to feel increasingly useless, which undermined her sense of self-worth. Eventually, things got so bad that she was forced to reassess her life and look for a new focus.

For Joanna, this was not easy. Since becoming a mother, she had never entertained the thought of a full-time career. After much self-analysis and discussion with her husband, however, she decided to turn her experience with children to good use and train as a nursery school teacher. "The pleasure and fulfillment I get from my work is more than I could ever have anticipated," she says now. "My horizons have broadened and I have gained a confidence that benefits every other area of my life."

Find a new direction

Peter had to change focus when an injury forced him to abandon a promising career as a dancer. At the time, it seemed the greatest tragedy; he was 23 and had never been seriously interested in anything else. Because he knew he didn't have enough experience to become a dance teacher or choreographer, he became seriously depressed. Then one day, while drawing with his niece, he found himself sketching a dancing figure. As

A new world…
Changing your focus can help you look at the world with fresh eyes, reawaken your vitality, and be highly stimulating.

he drew, not only was he aware that his feelings of depression and unhappiness were lifting, but he was reminded of how much he had enjoyed art lessons at school. He felt inspired to enrol for an art course, and took a degree in fine art. Now a successful painter, he recently spent six months as an artist in residence with a prestigious dance company. By transferring his passion for dance from the stage to the canvas, he gave his life new direction and meaning.

Keep yourself inspired

Trying to change your focus, particularly in a major way, can be a fraught and confusing business. You may feel as if one foot is edging tentatively toward the future while the other is stuck in the past. At these times, looking to someone else who has successfully navigated a course similar to your own can be very inspiring. It does not matter whether

Leaping ahead

Keeping an open mind and viewing changes as opportunities can help you turn setbacks into turning points; you can then forge ahead in a new direction.

you are inspired by people you know personally or have learned about from your friends or from newspapers, magazines, or television. The important thing is to analyze their attitudes and try to learn from them. If you are recently divorced, for example, you will be heartened to meet someone who has been through a divorce, overcome the pain, developed a positive outlook, and rebuilt a new and happier life. Similarly, if you are thinking about making a radical career change, hearing about someone else who has made such a change successfully can give you courage and hope.

CHANGE YOUR THINKING

The way you perceive the world is determined by your beliefs about yourself, others, and society as a whole. These beliefs create your attitude to life. They are the blueprint that determines how you behave, with whom you associate, what you try to achieve, and what you try to avoid. Positive beliefs frame your experiences in a hopeful and constructive light. By contrast, negative beliefs inhibit your potential for growth, and make you less ready to take advantage of opportunities.

Every word you speak and every action you take begins with a thought. If you believe that you are incapable of changing a particular view or way of behaving, you will think it is pointless to try and make no effort to do so—and because you make no effort, your conviction is proved correct. As many research studies have shown, belief in personal control, in your ability to influence the course of your life, is a key element in positive, productive thinking.

Jason's story illustrates this point. Constantly put down by his ambitious and demanding parents, Jason grew up thinking he was stupid, unimaginative, and useless. As a result, he left school at 16 with no qualifications and went to work in a supermarket, stacking shelves. He soon became frustrated and bored, however, and something inside him rebelled.

"Who says I'm useless? Who says I can't make something of my life?" he found himself thinking angrily. It was this thought, as well as the determination to prove his parents and teachers wrong, that motivated him to return to full-time education. He later went on to study history and law at university, and now has his own successful legal practice.

Acting the part

One of the most effective ways of changing the way you think is to behave as though it has changed already. Soon, your new beliefs will become like second nature to you, and you will start to feel and act accordingly. The positive responses you receive to your new behavior will reinforce it. If you want to boost your self-confidence, for example, practice acting like someone full of confidence and self-respect. This might mean standing up for yourself

in a situation when you would normally have kept silent, asking for the raise you think you deserve, or simply treating yourself to celebrate an achievement.

Similarly, if you want to become more optimistic, try to express more hopeful opinions about things you might instinctively view with suspicion. This doesn't mean blinding yourself to reality, but it does mean imagining a positive outcome. If you want to be more socially outgoing, act like an outgoing person and muster up the courage to initiate a conversation with a stranger at a party. Think of people you know whose qualities you would like to have, and recall or imagine how they would act.

LEARNING FROM FAILURE

A crucial aspect of positive thinking is your attitude to setbacks and failure. If you believe that you can learn from setbacks, then every situation can provide valuable insights that will help you move forward. Remember that successful people may make as many mistakes—or more—than those who are less successful; the difference is that they refuse to be discouraged when things go wrong, and continue to try out other possibilities. They know that you can learn as much from a failure as from a success. Whereas success is a confirmation that you have got something right, failure obliges you to analyze, reassess, question, or plan a new strategy; it shows you where you have gone wrong so that you can discover a fresh starting point.

Seeing the light

Thomas Edison, who patented more than 1,000 inventions, never allowed himself to become discouraged. When he was asked how it felt to have failed so many times in his efforts to produce an electric light bulb, he replied that he had not failed at all. He had been successful in finding thousands of ways of how *not* to make a light bulb! This positive, constructive attitude is one worth emulating. Persistence, in combination with inventiveness and the capacity and willingness to learn from experience, ultimately brought Edison's experiments to a successful conclusion, and you will find that these qualities can be effective for you, too.

A perfect model
Start the process of change by imitating the behavior of someone you admire; remind yourself that if he or she can do it, then so can you.

This is not as difficult as it might sound. In fact, you have probably done it instinctively many times. When you first started in a job, for example, you may well have "acted" being professional and proficient until you became more experienced. To some extent, a first-time mother also "plays" at motherhood until she becomes more confident and learns to trust in her ability to keep her child safe and protected.

Stick with it

At first, faking it may make you feel awkward and uncomfortable, but do persist; after all, your attitudes are the result of years of conditioning, and part of you will resist change. If you persevere, however, you will no longer suffer from self-defeating attitudes that sabotage your progress—you will open the door to a more rewarding and positive life.

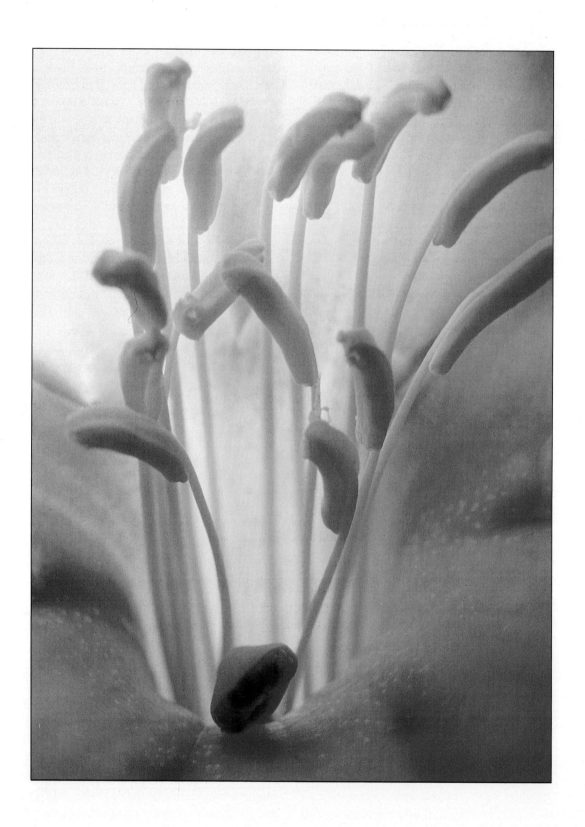

CHAPTER TWO

YOUR INNER SELF

AS WELL AS your "outer self," the "you" that you present to the world, you also have deeply rooted needs, desires, and aspirations. If you ignore the yearnings of your inner life, or if there is little harmony between your inner and outer self, it's possible you may feel unfulfilled and empty. Understanding who you are and what you want from life is essential for your personal development, and the quiz "Who Are You?" pages 34-35, will help you assess how in touch you are with your inner self. A second quiz, "Discover Your Real Needs," pages 36-37, will then guide you toward discovering what is most important or compelling to you.

Feelings can be a source of tremendous joy, but they can also seem so overwhelming that it may feel safer to try to keep them at bay. But suppressed feelings may simply resurface in other ways, undermining your health and well-being. "Get in Touch," pages 38-39, helps you to experience and express your hidden or buried feelings so that you can harness their energy toward appropriate goals. Similarly, "Know Your Own Mind," pages 40-41, illustrates the technique of "laddering"—where you use a series of questions to help reveal your deeply held, perhaps subconscious, beliefs.

Your long-term plans and goals may bring you great fulfillment, but don't lose sight of the rewards of everyday life. "Live for Today," pages 44-45, looks at the joys of spontaneity and the importance of making the most of the present. "Come to Your Senses," pages 46-47, explores another way you can live in the moment and feel more fully alive.

Do you have a fertile imagination? A rich mental life can aid relaxation, enhance your memory, help you in creative problem-solving, and provide an insight into your secret aspirations (see "Enhance Your Imagination," pp. 48-49). Your interests and leisure pursuits can also yield clues as to what will bring you fulfillment; they may reveal important personality traits and qualities, which you could perhaps use more fully in your work or even as a pointer to a new direction if you want to change your career (see "Tap Your Talents," pp. 52-53.)

While some people may have an outlet for their spirituality in organized religion, others may need to explore this aspect of themselves independently, and find their own way of connecting to a "higher self" or purpose. "Spiritual Peace," pages 60-61, discusses the importance of this often neglected side of our inner selves.

LOOKING DEEP INTO YOUR INNER SELF AND GETTING IN TOUCH

WITH YOUR TRUE FEELINGS CAN OPEN YOUR EYES TO

THE BEAUTY OF WHAT YOU HAVE TO OFFER THE WORLD.

WHO ARE YOU?

All of us want to "be ourselves," to feel a harmony between our inner reality and the world around us. We want to express our own individuality, rather than conform to the expectations of others. Modern life, however, is a noisy and distracting affair. Quiet moments are few and far between, and staying in touch with who we are and what we truly desire is often hard. This questionnaire will help you find out if you are in touch with your inner self; for results, turn to page 139.

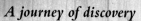

for results, turn to page 139.

A journey of discovery
Exploring your inner self and the hidden recesses of your personality will help you to understand yourself better, and to be more in touch with what you want in life.

1. How often do you spend time thinking about how, and why, your life has turned out as it has?
a) Once a week.
b) Every now and then.
c) Never.

2. Do you agree with those who say introspection is self-indulgent and stops people getting on with life?
a) Not at all.
b) To some degree.
c) Absolutely.

3. How often do you feel satisfied and fulfilled at the end of the day?
a) Very often.
b) It goes in phases according to what's going on.
c) Rarely—I'm mostly tired and stressed out, and have to try to relax so I can face the next day.

4. If someone asked what you value most about yourself, would you be able to answer?
a) With no difficulty.
b) I'd have to think about it.
c) Probably not.

5. If you have a day free of chores and obligations, do you know how to spend it?
a) Always.
b) I sometimes feel at a loose end.
c) No, I feel on edge and restless; I'm afraid of wasting time, but feel I should just relax.

6. How often do you give yourself a day free of chores and obligations?
a) At every opportunity.
b) When there's something I really want to do.
c) Never.

7. If you remember your dreams, do you ever write them down and try to analyze them?
a) Often—I keep a dream diary.
b) Only if a dream has left a particularly strong impression.
c) Never, dreams don't interest me.

8. Are you comfortable if a friend or loved one asks you to share your inner feelings?
a) Yes, completely.
b) It depends on the circumstances and my mood.
c) No, I feel invaded and irritable.

9. Are your choices determined by what you want or believe, rather than by outside pressure or habit?
a) Frequently.
b) Not as often as I would like.
c) Rarely.

10. Do books on personal growth interest you?
a) Yes, I'm very interested.
b) I'm somewhat interested.
c) I have no interest at all.

11. Do you sometimes react in a way you are unprepared for and don't understand?
a) Almost never.
b) Sometimes.
c) Frequently.

12. Do you ever feel your life has become an "uncomfortable fit" or that you're not "real"?
a) Only in situations that force me to behave like someone I'm not.
b) Every now and then.
c) Often.

13. How often do you catch glimpses of the child you once were?
a) Very often.
b) Once in a while when I'm feeling particularly carefree or relaxed, or am spontaneous.
c) Never.

14. Do you feel comfortable with silence?
a) Yes, it allows me to listen to my thoughts.
b) Only when I'm in a tranquil mood.
c) No, silence unnerves me.

15. What do you think of the statement: "We are not troubled by things, but the opinion we have of things"?
a) I agree completely.
b) It's not always that cut and dried.
c) I disagree.

DISCOVER YOUR REAL NEEDS

WHAT DO WE NEED for a happy, successful life? We know that we have certain physical needs for water, air, food, shelter, and sleep in order to survive, and from an early age we know how important it is to meet those needs. As children, we cry for attention; as adults, we learn to meet these needs ourselves. However, we often overlook what psychologists believe is just as important to our well-being: the ability to understand our emotional needs. It is only by knowing what makes us happy that we can incorporate specific, meaningful goals into our lives, and adapt our behavior in order to get what we want.

Don't be too needy

Your superficial needs—those that bring you short-term gratification, such as a new outfit—may be very different from your deeper needs, such as a meaningful career or a happy relationship, and it is easy to confuse the two. In order to sustain your well-being and self-esteem, you have to learn to recognize which needs are essential to fulfill and which are distracting you from achieving your potential. Certain needs, such as those below, can work against you if they become exaggerated.

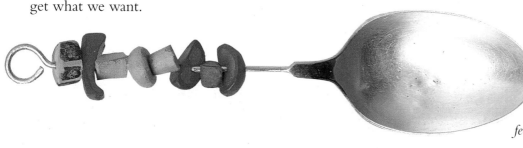

• **Food:** *While everyone needs to eat, and many of us enjoy the pleasures of food, repeated comfort bingeing or stringent starvation diets can indicate that you may feel unloved and lonely.*

• **Sex:** *Compulsively seeking sex may be a way to relieve loneliness, or to compensate for other feelings of failure.*

• **Attention:** *Everyone needs to be acknowledged and loved, which we express by paying attention to someone. People who are insecure or who suffer from low self-esteem may constantly seek attention in immature ways, such as hypochondria.*

• **Money:** *It's important to be financially responsible for yourself, but to value or "rank" yourself or other people only by their income or possessions is ungenerous and self-defeating. Do you enjoy what you already have? Many people are discovering they have greater peace of mind with less money than they had with higher earnings but a high-stress job.*

Changing needs and "fire-fighting"

It is important to recognize that you have different needs at different times in your life. When you were a child, for example, you probably needed a great deal of attention from people who helped keep you safe, but as you get older, you become increasingly self-reliant.

If you ignore your changing needs, your life may become a series of crises as you race around trying to cope: behavior that psychologists call "fire-fighting." In fact, you may unconsciously create dramas as a way of avoiding an issue in your life that should be acknowledged or resolved. Fire-fighting may result from hanging on to a situation that hinders, rather than encourages, your individuality. Once you understand your needs and what is important to you, you can begin to organize your life by establishing a list of priorities. You are then on the path to controlling your destiny.

Sarah, for example, had recently started work for a famous publishing house, and was disappointed to discover how boring her supposedly glamorous job had turned out. Her confidence and self-esteem were slowly eroded by her work, and she focused all her feelings of failure on her small apartment, which she began to hate: If only she had space, she thought, or if only she lived in a different part of the city, or could change the decor of her apartment, her life would be so much better. When a friend pointed out how Sarah had confused her needs—and that her frustrating job was the real issue—Sarah realized that she would be better off redirecting her energy into finding a better position, and, after doing so, completely forgot about moving house.

Put first things first

One way to become more aware of your needs is to write them down. Look, too, at your motives, desires, and ambitions. This exercise allows you to clarify and balance your needs, to discover those that are most important, those that may be unrealistic or impractical, and to commit yourself to meeting those that would best contribute to self-fulfillment. Initially, this task might be difficult or confusing, but by getting to know yourself and identifying what you want, balancing your needs becomes easier. You'll experience greater contentment, and feel more confident about your future.

START WITH THE BASICS

How do you recognize your real needs? In his book *How to Get What You Want Out of Life*, author William J. Reilly divides needs into four areas, and poses simple questions to help you focus your thoughts:

1. Money: How much do you need in order to live the way you want to?

2. Love: What kind of relationships do you want?

3. Ego food: What things make you feel good?

4. Health: How will you maintain it?

Most of your more complex needs probably fall under these broad headings; expand each category by asking yourself more specific questions. For example, "ego food" includes your spiritual, creative, and intellectual needs, so you might consider whether having your work provide mental challenges is more important to you than prestige. "Love" includes family and friends as well as partners; ask yourself what degree of intimacy you feel comfortable with, or whether you prefer being part of a large group of friends or just having two or three close intimates.

Using these four categories as the foundation for greater self-awareness, you can start to pinpoint the area where your greatest need is—perhaps the one that demands your most urgent attention.

Distorted needs

Your superficial needs may distort or obscure much deeper, more important needs, leaving you feeling empty and dissatisfied. Try to focus on what is essential.

GET IN TOUCH

FEELINGS are a very complex combination of emotions, perceptions, and bodily sensations. They color how you see the world, and are the means by which you become conscious of your intuitive responses to life events. When you're happy and feeling positive, for example, everything looks rosy and life seems great. When you experience emotions such as sadness or frustration, however, the world probably looks bleak. How you respond to or express your feelings is a measure of self-acceptance: If you think you cannot or are not "allowed" to be yourself, or that your feelings are somehow unacceptable, your life may never be truly your own, and you will block yourself from fulfilling your potential. To feel is to participate in life and to be alive.

Reconnecting: a source of power
Feelings of anxiety, or of being detached or ineffectual, may be due to buried emotions or fears; once they are acknowledged or expressed, you will probably feel a surge of vitality as you connect with your "real" self.

How feelings become blocked
Feelings are controlled—and sometimes completely blocked—in two ways: suppression and repression. Suppression results from a conscious decision not to think about something unpleasant, uncomfortable, or unacceptable; you may, for example, suspect that your partner is having an affair but push your suspicions away because you don't want to think about it, much less confront him or her. Repression, on the other hand, is an unconscious protective device, which, by definition, you don't know you're doing. For example, a young woman might claim that she doesn't want to get married on principle, but may not recognize an unconscious fear as a reaction to her parents' unhappy marriage.

The perils of suppression
Although we may sometimes try to squash down our feelings because a part of ourselves finds them too painful to face, this can be potentially destructive. As babies, we expressed our every emotion and need as we felt it: If we were hungry or wanted attention, we cried. As we grow older, however, we learn not to express ourselves as spontaneously as we once did, and our feelings can become separated from who we think we are (our ego identity). Psychologists recognize the peril of constant suppression of strong feelings—especially of what we think of as negative emotions, such as anger—and believe that this is a factor in triggering depression, stress-related conditions such as high blood pressure and ulcers, and even illnesses such as cancer.

Strong feelings do not evaporate if we ignore them: They become buried deep inside us, sometimes with dramatic consequences to our physical and emotional well-being. When Mary's father

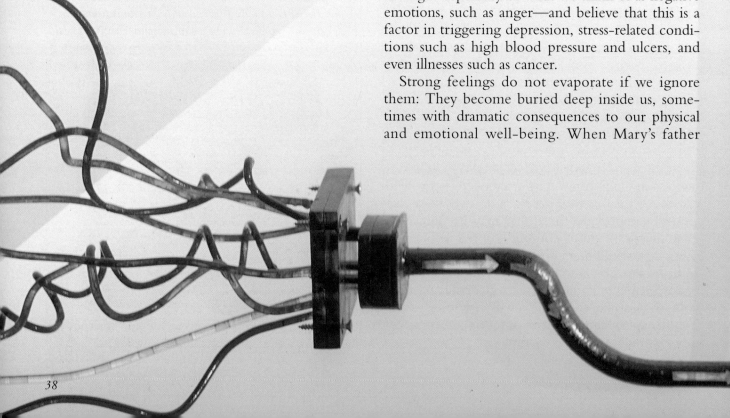

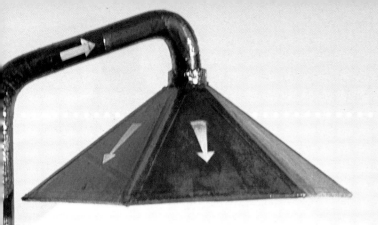

GETTING STARTED

The following practical exercises can help you gain insight into your feelings in a safe, secure way. Remember to be gentle with yourself, take your time, and do not judge yourself. If you find certain deeply buried feelings too difficult to face, you might want to talk to a sensitive, trusted friend, or consider seeing a professional counselor.

• First, find a place where you feel safe and will not be disturbed. If there is an event or memory that saddens or angers you, focus on it, and allow your feelings about it to surface.

• If you feel anxious, you can use relaxation and breathing techniques to help you unwind.

• If you're angry, try addressing yourself in the mirror or speak to an empty chair, imagining that you're telling the person who has angered you why you feel the way you do. If you feel like expressing your anger physically, get some pillows and hit them.

• If your feelings are too painful to articulate, write them down or draw them.

• Meditation techniques will help you learn to focus your mind and overcome certain negative emotions, such as resentment.

• Learn how to recognize your mood changes. Become aware of what kind of situations or behavior trigger particular feelings in you.

• Trust that it is in your interests to discover what your real feelings are.

died unexpectedly, everyone marveled at her composure. She did not shed a tear, even during the funeral service, and was a source of endless comfort to her mother and siblings. In fact, she had cut herself off from the enormity of her loss, and buried her feelings so deeply that long after the funeral, when she had the time and the space to begin to cope with her bereavement, she found herself unable to cry and thus assumed that she had resolved her grief.

About a year later, however, Mary's pet dog was killed by a car, and she was inconsolable; she wept for days, which surprised and worried her friends. The shock of her dog's death had brought all her buried feelings about her father's death back to the surface with an intensity that overwhelmed her, and it took many months for her to integrate this major loss into her life and come to terms with it. Wisely, Mary thought bereavement counseling would help, and after six months felt that the most intense period of mourning had slowly lifted.

Get back in touch with your feelings

How can you rediscover your buried emotions? First, you must learn to feel comfortable with your feelings, whatever they are; if you resent your colleague's promotion, for example, admit to yourself that you are angry and jealous, but accept that these feelings of being hurt or unrecognized are not unnatural. By being honest with yourself, and recognizing your true feelings, you can reach a point of self-acceptance and self-forgiveness. As Louise L. Hay says in her book *The Power Is Within You*, "What you can feel you can heal." Hay recognizes that, when emotions surface, there might be tears and anger, which have to be resolved or "worked through." To make the process easier, she suggests you repeat to yourself:
• "I now release with ease all old negative beliefs."
• "It's comfortable for me to change."
• "My pathway is now smooth."
• "I am free of the past."

By using this technique, it is possible to learn how to be resilient, cultivate insight, and maintain inner calm. You may also discover that even negative emotions serve a purpose: They will stimulate you to outgrow your limitations on your journey to becoming a more honest, authentic person.

KNOW YOUR OWN MIND

Self-awareness and understanding are essential for personal development, so it is important to take time to deepen your understanding of yourself. Asking yourself why you feel or behave in a certain way will help you begin to discover what your real feelings and beliefs are.

Laddering

Trying to find out more about your inner fears and deepest motivations can be difficult. Long-term psychoanalysis or therapy might help you to gain access to your more buried feelings, but many people don't have the time, money, or inclination for this. One technique that you might want to consider is "laddering," which derives from the idea that a basic statement, such as "I feel guilty when I miss church on Sunday," can be explored through a series of pertinent questions in order to discover the hidden or unconscious source of the feeling—as well as the underlying motivation—expressed by the statement. A sample question session begins at the base of the ladder (below right):

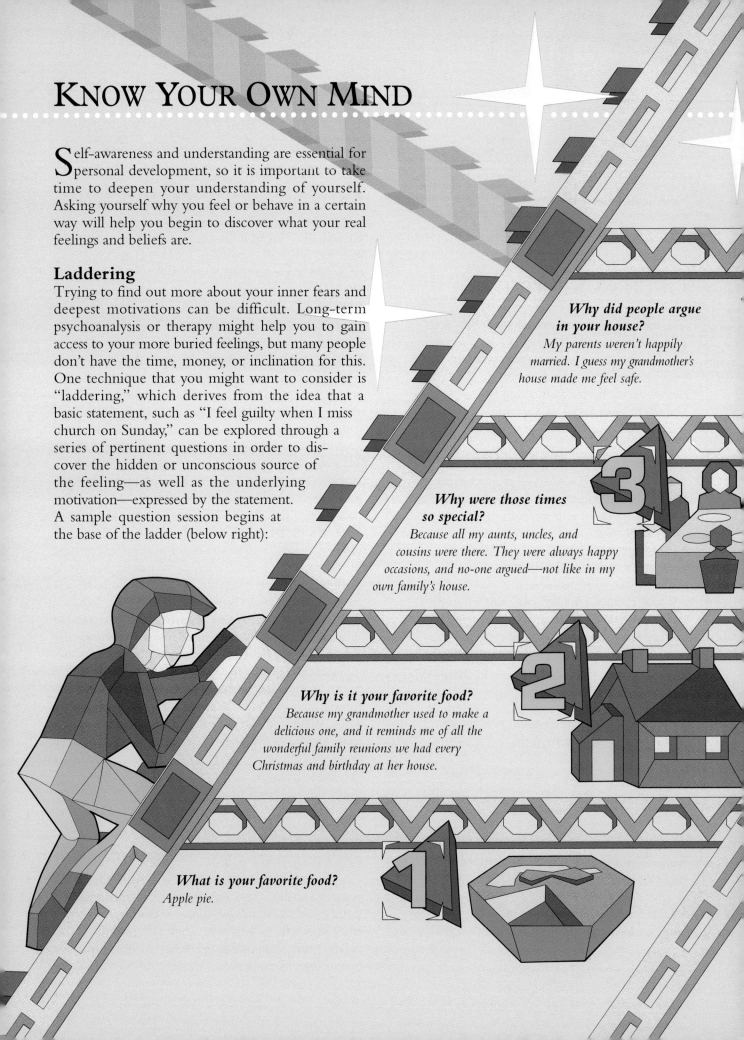

Why did people argue in your house?
My parents weren't happily married. I guess my grandmother's house made me feel safe.

Why were those times so special?
Because all my aunts, uncles, and cousins were there. They were always happy occasions, and no-one argued—not like in my own family's house.

Why is it your favorite food?
Because my grandmother used to make a delicious one, and it reminds me of all the wonderful family reunions we had every Christmas and birthday at her house.

What is your favorite food?
Apple pie.

Trying it out

To illustrate how laddering works, here are two different ways someone might respond to one specific question. Remember that there are as many different answers as there are people, and that you could go on asking many more questions, or entirely different ones.

Question: *Where would you prefer to live, in a city or in the country?*
Answer 1: I prefer the country.
Why?
Because you can get to know who your neighbors are more easily, and develop a sense of living in a close community.
Why is it important to know your neighbors?
Because when you're in trouble, you may need help; in a city, nobody knows who lives next door.
Why might you be in trouble?
I might need advice about local services, or need someone to let in the electrician while I'm at work; when we're in trouble, or if there were an intruder, it helps to know you can trust your neighbors. We all need to depend on each other
Why do we need to depend on each other?
Because otherwise we'd all be completely isolated and alone, and that would be frightening and unbearable. I need other people.

Answer 2: I prefer the country.
Why?
Because of the wide-open spaces and peacefulness.
Why do you like that?
Because no-one would bother me.
Why is that important to you?
In a city, there are so many people making a lot of noise, you don't have time to be alone or to think.
Why do you need time to think?
I need to reflect on myself and the direction of my life; I don't like feeling that I'm just drifting along, overwhelmed by people and events.

A word of caution

Laddering is not a process you should enter into lightly; indeed, psychologist and writer Dorothy Rowe, who explains laddering in her book *The Successful Self*, stresses that it is not a game, and should be used with care because very strong feelings may surface. People who are already deeply troubled should not try laddering except in the safe context of counseling or therapy.

THE MIND-BODY CONNECTION

FOR THOUSANDS OF YEARS, Eastern philosophies have emphasized the idea that happiness and well-being can be achieved by maintaining a harmonious balance between mind and body. Yet it is only recently in the West that we have come to appreciate the significance of this idea. As alarm bells start to ring about our increasingly stressful and sedentary lifestyle, more and more people are waking up to the fact that we need to take a holistic approach to our well-being; that is, we need to see the mind and the body as interdependent. Health and tranquility cannot be achieved by treating one or the other in isolation.

Radiant mind and body
Certain disciplines such as yoga help keep your body healthy and flexible, and also contribute to clarity of mind and tranquility.

Don't neglect your body

There are numerous body-based Eastern approaches that bring about a harmonious integration of mind and body. Two of the best known are yoga and t'ai chi, but almost any form of exercise will benefit you: Exercise encourages deep breathing, which, in turn, increases the circulation of freshly oxygenated blood. It also increases the production of "feel-good" chemicals such as endorphins, which are the body's natural painkillers.

But it is not just the body that responds positively to this enlivening activity. The mind also becomes more alert. One of the main reasons for this is that the brain functions best when it is well oxygenated—taking any form of mildly strenuous exercise will increase the supply of freshly oxygenated blood to the brain by about 20 percent. This partially explains why desk-bound staff often feel so exhausted at the end of a working day—their brains are starved of oxygen!

Many people have attested to the benefits of exercise on their ability to think creatively. The Scottish inventor James Watt, for example, recalled that his triumphant flash of inspiration, which would improve his basic steam engine design, occurred while he was taking a Sunday afternoon constitutional in 1765: "I had not walked farther than the golf house when the whole thing was arranged in my mind!" Some physiologists think that exercise stimulates the brain to produce alpha waves, which result in a more relaxed state of mind and calm alertness. It is also possible that what people experience during an inspirational moment when they solve a problem all at once is a shift from the logical left side of the brain to the more intuitive right hemisphere of the brain—a shift that is more easily achieved when the brain is relaxed, rather than overfocused on details.

Numerous studies strongly indicate that taking some form of regular exercise helps you to feel more relaxed and confident, and to have a greater sense of being at one with yourself. The Canadian Dr. Tom Stephens, commenting on a fitness survey of the United States and Canada, went as far as to say: "The inescapable conclusion is that physical activity is positively associated with good mental health, especially positive mood, general well-being, and less anxiety and depression."

Don't forget your mind!

As well as being aware of our bodies, we need to pay attention to our thoughts and feelings. Happy thoughts, it seems, have a positive effect on the body, while chronic negative states such as worry, anger, or resentment may weaken the immune system, leaving us more vulnerable to illness. As Dr. Deepak Chopra observes in his book *Creating Health*, happiness causes "biochemical changes in the brain that in turn have profoundly beneficial effects on the body's physiology." He then adds, "Sad or depressing thoughts…have a detrimental effect." There is increasing medical evidence to support this claim. Dr. Chopra cites the example of an unusual disorder

The best connection
Showing affection by holding someone close, or by simply smiling, reduces stress, encourages joy, and promotes mutual well-being.

known as psychosocial dwarfism in children who have suffered from long-term emotional deprivation at home. The growth of these children is stunted—up to 50 percent less than the average for their age group. When the children are removed to a more loving and supportive environment, they start to grow again—in other words, their body chemistry adjusts back to healthy levels in response to emotional warmth and care. Although this is a dramatic instance of the effect of unhappiness on physical health, the message is that vitality and joy depend to a great extent on appreciating and responding to the needs of both your mind and body, and maintaining a happy balance.

KEEPING YOUR BALANCE

In order to pay attention to the needs of your body and mind, and to maintain optimum well-being, try to incorporate these elements into your daily life:
• **Relaxation:** Take a few moments during the day to breathe deeply. Let your mind wander, or focus on a pleasant memory or a restful, inner landscape.
• **Exercise:** Walking and swimming are two forms of exercise that are extremely beneficial. Remember, you don't have to compete with anyone—simply enjoy yourself.
• **Posture:** Improving your posture helps the body to function more efficiently, and encourages happy, positive thoughts. Try this interesting experiment. Slouch down in your chair and hang your head down.

After a few minutes, observe your thoughts. Perhaps you've started to think about various worries and concerns, and feel low. Now think about something that makes you feel good, a recent success or pleasurable event. Do you feel as though you want to change the position of your body?
• **Affirmations:** Positive statements that you say out loud or silently to yourself—such as, "I am loving and lovable," or "My body is strong and healthy"—all help to encourage well-being.
• **Visualization:** Use your mind's eye to "visualize" an improved state of mind or health. With your eyes closed, see yourself full of health and vigor, confident and smiling, and eager to face the future.

LIVE FOR TODAY

Our society is extremely goal-oriented, and from an early age we're encouraged to strive for achievement, from winning races to passing examinations. As we go through life, many of us continue to set ourselves targets, ranging from long-term goals, such as what we want from our career, to more short-term, day-to-day concerns. We admire those who have achieved financial, academic, career, and social success, and too often we evaluate our own achievements solely in these terms. Our goals become projects to be completed, necessary tasks that we feel we *should* do, rather than things we really want to do. We channel all our energies into chasing goals and become blinkered to what is happening around us. In this way, striving for goals can have a detrimental effect, reducing our enjoyment of the present, making us less spontaneous, and shutting us off from wider opportunities and alternative paths.

Enjoy getting there

It is not necessarily the goals themselves that are restrictive. Indeed, many people find that they are motivated by setting personal challenges, for without them, they might just drift aimlessly through life. Although it is important to have goals, remember that by constantly striving for what is just beyond your reach, you may become dissatisfied with what you already have. Working all hours, for example, may lead you to neglect your health or your family, and there is no guarantee that your effort will be rewarded. Even if you achieve your goal, you might not feel fulfilled.

Remind yourself of the adage: "It's the journey that's important, not the destination." Set aside time for yourself that does not involve having to be productive or working toward a particular aim; try reading or listening to music. Allow yourself the leisure to enjoy simply being alive, and remember that regardless of where you are headed, today is as important as tomorrow.

Don't rush through life
Take time to enjoy the present. Blindly pursuing your goals is like traveling the world without appreciating each distinctive culture or country.

MAKING THE MOST OF THE PRESENT

If you're constantly looking ahead and striving for what you don't have, much of the enjoyment of the present will pass you by. When you eat a meal, for example, you should not aim solely to satisfy your hunger, but also to enjoy the taste and textures. Try to think of life itself as a meal of varied flavors, each of which you should take the time to savor and enjoy. By being open and receptive to the present—new angles, ideas, and approaches—you're more likely to discover what really makes you happy, and you will also find a lasting, deeper success. The six points below will help you to do this:

• **Keep things in perspective.** Have confidence in your abilities and use them to the full. Setting yourself challenges can be motivating and positive, but make sure your aims are realistic and achievable.

• **Clarify and balance your aims.** Be clear about what is important to you *now*, as well as what you want later in life. If you think you will not be able to maintain a balance between the two, you might consider other possibilities.

• **Don't compare yourself with others.** Although what others achieve should inspire you, you should still set your own standards and follow them through.

• **Be open to experience.** Don't judge everything only in terms of success and failure. By aiming to achieve a qualification, for example, realize that it is not just the piece of paper bearing your name that will be valuable. It is the process of learning and the experiences you gain along the way. If you fail an exam, don't discount the experience as worthless; if you have learned something, it is valuable.

• **Live for the moment.** Learn to appreciate what you already have rather than always looking for something else. Today is an unrepeatable day during which you can enjoy, create, or achieve a great deal.

• **Do it for yourself.** Begin a project or plan a change because you really want to—not simply because you feel you should or that it is expected of you. You're more likely to achieve your aims if you really want something, rather than undertaking the task halfheartedly.

Carpe diem—"seize the day"
This Latin saying is a reminder that life is short, and that each day is a precious gift that brings an opportunity to make of it what you will.

Come to Your Senses

So much of our time is spent getting to where we want to go, focusing on the end result, that we tend to leave little room for the simpler pleasures of life—the minute-to-minute enjoyment of our physical, sensuous, and sensual selves. But if you live your life dwelling on the past or worrying about the future, you'll never actually live it in the present.

What's happening now?

Almost all of us, to a greater or lesser degree, are encouraged to "live in our heads" as we struggle to organize our increasingly complex or office-bound lives. Does this describe you? If so, you may be in danger of losing touch with a vital part of yourself—your body—and may be missing out on a pleasurable sense of vital alertness and "nowness" that cannot be experienced by the intellect alone.

Enjoy your surroundings
Take the time to appreciate the sights, sounds, textures, tastes, and smells of your world—just indulge your senses.

Stop reading at the end of this sentence, and pause to reflect on the physical sensations you have been aware of in the last few minutes. Unless you had a pain somewhere in your body, perhaps you noticed nothing at all. Now put the book down, relax, and simply experience where you are right now, without "doing" anything with your mind—that is, without thinking. What can you see, feel, hear, taste, smell? You will appreciate your senses more—and the sensations they provide—if you exercise them regularly, especially if your life is very busy or your work is mentally challenging.

Learn to focus

The following "sensate-focus" exercises will help you rediscover each sense in turn, allowing you to put aside the habit of thinking about the world around you so that you can experience and feel it instead. During each exercise, try to clear your mind of other thoughts, and simply turn your attention to one specific sense. Words and thoughts—mental chatter—will probably creep into your consciousness, but gently push them away and "come to your senses" again.

Sight: Take a few minutes to stop and look at a tree. Notice the shape of the leaves, and the patterns they form with the branches, and how these change as the wind stirs and then dies down again. Look at the color and texture of the leaves. Are they different colors, matte or shiny, smooth or ribbed? Notice the effect of light and shade, the play of shadows, and how translucent the leaves look when the sun is behind them. What else can you see?

Touch: The sensation of touch registers not only texture, but also warmth, cold, pressure, and even pain. We use touch to demonstrate affection, tenderness, or concern. Animals, too, are highly responsive to touch; the next time you meet a friendly pet cat, dog, or rabbit, stroke the animal's fur with your fingers. Explore the contours of its shape, and be aware of how it is responding to you.

Taste: To get the most out of your sense of taste, you also need to use your nose. Take an orange and sniff it. Now cut into it—does the scent intensify as the skin is pierced? Put a segment in your mouth, but don't bite into it. Explore its shape and texture with your tongue, then chew it slowly, savoring the juice. Now taste a completely different food, one with a contrasting texture, such as whipped cream. Savor each food slowly.

Smell: You may only be aware of smells when they are particularly strong or distinctive, such as the aroma of freshly made coffee or newly cut grass, or the chlorine odor of a swimming pool. Smells can have a powerful effect on our mood:

simply inhale the scent of a flower such as rose, jasmine, or hyacinth, or enjoy a deep bath perfumed with a few drops of lavender oil. Grow herbs such as rosemary, mint, and marjoram in your garden or window box, and rub the leaves gently to release their fragrance. Is each smell sharp, sweet, or pungent? Notice if the different smells make you feel tranquil or energetic.

Hearing: Closing your eyes helps you become more aware of the sounds around you. Focus on sounds only for a few minutes. If you are at home, what do you hear: People talking? Birdsong? Traffic? Children playing? Music? At the beach, listen to the sound the waves make as they lap the shore or crash against the rocks. What is the rhythm like? Is it a gentle sound, or full of raw energy? Is it restful or stimulating?

Next steps

You can also try using your body in new ways, such as walking more briskly or learning some form of dance, and increase your awareness of the pleasures of the natural world by taking time to stop and notice what's around you—the weather, the sky, the stars at night, the rustling of leaves in the wind. All these exercises will help you to enlarge your perceptions, and to appreciate the world around you and your relationship to it.

SIMPLE PLEASURES

Don't waste your senses—they can be a source of great pleasure. Here are a few simple suggestions:
• Indulge in a sensuous breakfast in bed: flaky croissant or crusty bread, succulent apricot jam, tangy fruit juice or fresh coffee, juicy melon or grapefruit, scrambled eggs. Prepare the tray with a cloth napkin and a scented flower in a vase.
• Take some form of regular exercise that you enjoy—go for a swim or run, or try squash, hill walking, or some kind of dancing.
• Food is a great stimulus. Take time to enjoy preparing a healthy meal. Notice the colors, textures and smells, and savor the tastes of the end result at a leisurely pace.
• Take turns with a partner to massage each other with different materials: velvet, angora, satin, toweling, a feather, then drizzle a little warm scented massage oil along his or her spine.

ENHANCE YOUR IMAGINATION

POSSIBLY THE GREATEST TREASURE of the human mind is the imagination: it enables us to create new solutions to problems, transcend the limitations of our everyday world, and reach for the magical and sublime. Although you may think that imagination is the preserve of artists and geniuses rather than "ordinary" people, in fact we all have this astounding and infinite capacity to dream, daydream, fantasize, or simply speculate about life, other people, or plans for the future.

The tremendous intellectual growth that occurs during the first six years of a child's life is greatly helped by his or her vivid and fertile imagination. As every parent knows, games of make-believe come naturally to children. A cardboard box, for example, is not just a box: It becomes a boat, a car,

Transforming your everyday world
The most ordinary aspects of your life may be doorways to a more imaginative realm. Fantasies need not serve any other purpose other than the joy of exploring your own mind.

a house, or a hideaway. A stick is transformed into a sword or magic wand, bright buttons and beads into secret treasure, an old curtain into a wizard's cloak. So profound and revealing is this capacity for transformation that psychologists use "play therapy" to discover the problems that children cannot talk about directly. Although the joy of intense and boundless imaginative activity seems to diminish as we grow older, it can be kept alive and flourishing by creating opportunities for "flights of fancy."

desires? The question, "What if…?" can also trigger imaginative reveries: "What if I left the city and moved to the country?" or "What if I spent six months traveling the world?" can be used to prompt discoveries about who you are.

Live a vivid life

Exercising your imagination may seem little more than an entertaining pastime, but it can also give birth to great achievements. Einstein, who as a child was a slow learner, said, "Imagination is more important than knowledge," and recognized that this astonishing ability can be an important key to creative problem-solving. He himself had insights about the nature of time, space, and relativity by taking mental trips to the stars and planets.

You can also use your imagination to enhance your memory; consider how readily a striking or bizarre image sticks in your mind compared with a boring one. Many memory-improvement exercises suggest using imaginative associations and pictures in your head to help you remember things.

Your imagination is a valuable aid to relaxation, self-confidence, and personal development, too: It is the basis of creative visualization—you can transport yourself to a wave-lapped shore or peaceful sanctuary when you want to relax, or you can picture yourself behaving confidently. Remember, in your imagination, you *can* be whoever you want.

Let your mind wander

If you have ever fantasized about winning a fortune or living on a desert island, you are already using your imagination! Keep stretching and using it: Create a fictional life for someone you don't know— a man on a bus or a woman in a café. Ask yourself questions about them: What kind of life does he have? What are his interests? What is her home like? What does she do? Let your imagination roam— your speculations don't have to be at all realistic, and may even be more enjoyable for being fanciful.

Another way of exercising your imagination is to play with inkblots or look at clouds drifting by, looking for shapes and pictures. Try to be aware of what thoughts and feelings occur to you. Are there any meaningful messages? Are the images you see realistic? Are they symbolic of buried hopes or

Find your medium

There are many ways to explore your imagination: if you feel you can't paint pictures on paper, for example, close your eyes and paint one in your head instead.

FANTASY OR FIXATION?

Fantasies can brighten up our lives, help pass the time when we are bored, sustain us through difficult times, and provide us with insights into our secret wishes and desires. They can help us live out a dream that is unlikely to be realized—for example, a teenager might dream of being a pop star, or an aspiring musician might dream of playing to a packed concert hall—and can also enhance real life: Research shows that fantasizing is often a normal part of a healthy sex life.

For the most part, fantasies are pleasant and harmless diversions, but they also serve a useful purpose: By helping us to acknowledge our aspirations and understand more about who we would like to be, they can then stimulate and inspire us to make real changes in our lives.

The dark side

Although fantasies are certainly enjoyable, there is a risk that they can become a way of avoiding problems, a refuge from the real world. When fantasies are indulged in obsessively, and become the most satisfying part of your life, they can make it harder to create a fulfilling *real* life. For example, Craig had always been shy and withdrawn, and his fantasies reflected his frustrated need for praise, admiration, and attention. He fantasized about saving a child from drowning, rescuing a neighbor from a burning house, confronting armed robbers, and so on. Initially, his fantasies were harmless and not time-consuming. Gradually, however, they became more vivid than his unsatisfactory reality, and he found himself returning to them again and again during

IS THE GRASS GREENER?

Do you always dream about what you don't have? While fantasies can be fun, they can also inhibit your ability to enjoy the life you've already created for yourself, and prevent you from living it to the full. Ask yourself the following questions:
• Do you feel fulfilled and stimulated by your work and/or interests?
• Do you have relationships and friendships that you find rewarding and fun?
• Do you enjoy the simple pleasures of everyday life —walking or swimming, cooking and eating a leisurely meal, talking with family members or friends, playing games, or listening to music?

If your answer is "no" to any of these questions, you may be closing yourself off from enjoying your life, even in quite simple ways. Consider how you could devote some time and attention to cultivating these pleasures in your life.

Dreaming of the other side
If the grass always seems greener on the other side of the fence, and you find yourself continually fantasizing about leading a very different life, you need to work at either accepting the life you have—or taking action to change it.

Now ask yourself another set of questions:
• Do you tend to envy other people a lot?
• Do you spend much time thinking, "If only..."?
• Do you believe you could be outstanding or brilliant in a particular career if you only made the effort? Do you find you don't make time to study or to pursue your interests seriously?

If you answered "yes" to these questions, you may be overindulging your fantasy life at the expense of your real life. Work on making your life as you would like it to be—instead of using up your energy on unsatisfying or impossible dreams.

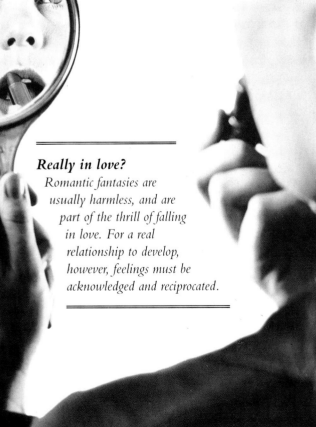

the day. Soon, the divide between fact and fiction had become blurred in his mind and he started telling people about his various feats, believing that they had actually happened. At this point, his family realized that he needed help, and persuaded him to have counseling. As a result, he was able to face the overwhelming need for attention and approval that prompted his excessively heroic fantasies in the first place.

Check your fantasies

If indulging in fantasies prevents you from changing your life, you might need to rein them in. If, instead of dealing with the difficulties in your relationship, for example, you retreat into fantasies of running off with your neighbor, then the fantasy is unhelpful. Focusing on the fantasy might also blind you to the many exciting challenges, pleasures, and joys of reality, or what your current relationship offers.

Miranda, for example, was obsessively infatuated with a colleague at work, convinced that when he nodded at her in the elevator it was a sign of his secret love. One day she discovered he was getting married. Distraught, she feigned a migraine and went home. Later that evening, a friend suggested to Miranda that her fantasy was largely the result of boredom at work; her friend encouraged Miranda to focus on expanding her job skills and changing her life for the better.

There's no need to exclude fantasies from your life, however, or to worry about them. Knowing how to enjoy them as harmless diversions and aids to greater self-knowledge and insight —without letting them take over your life—can keep your mind lively. You can then concentrate your energy and attention on what your real life has to offer—and on making some of your fantasies come true.

Really in love?
Romantic fantasies are usually harmless, and are part of the thrill of falling in love. For a real relationship to develop, however, feelings must be acknowledged and reciprocated.

TAP YOUR TALENTS

IS YOUR HOBBY absorbing and fun? Perhaps you've developed a high degree of skill or expertise in a special interest, and it is now very important to you; or perhaps your hobby is still rather peripheral, but you would like to devote more time to it. Whatever your hobby is—whether it's carpentry or white-water rafting, or something you do with like-minded friends or devote time to on your own—it probably provides an outlet for those personality traits and skills that you don't or can't express in your regular work or home environment. A hobby is not just a way to express qualities you already have, however; it can also be a way of stretching your imagination, cultivating completely different skills, and exploring new aspects of yourself.

Know your qualities

By looking closely at other people's leisure pursuits, you'll probably find vital clues about what really makes them tick, but the very fact that these pursuits are so important may be why they don't want to take them further: They may be afraid of putting themselves to the test and failing. Does this sound familiar? Have *you* ever secretly considered turning your own hobby into a career? Even if you haven't, you will benefit from considering just why you enjoy it, and what it reveals about you. The answers may point toward an aspect of yourself that might flourish and be developed in your daily job. For example, if you sail in your spare time, and you discover that you enjoy it partly because of the stimulating teamwork, then you might want to move into a position at work where you're part of a team. Alternatively, you might decide that working alone but enjoying a sport with others provides the right balance for you. Whatever you decide, don't dismiss your pastimes—they reveal a vital part of yourself as well as where your real talents may lie.

GETTING STARTED

If you have sometimes daydreamed about your hobby becoming a way of life, but fear taking the risk, perhaps you have a pessimistic inner voice that tells you the following things:

• I'm not really good enough at it.
• If it were my job, all the joy would go out of it.
• I wouldn't be relaxed doing it anymore, and it would stifle the skill I've enjoyed developing.
• It's something I do for myself, by myself; I use it to relax and I don't want to share it with others.
• What would I do as a hobby instead?
• It's not something I could turn into a "proper" job and earn money from.
• I couldn't earn a decent living at it.

How can you overcome your fear? If you have an intuition that you would like to risk making more of your hobby, you need to consider these two questions very carefully:

1. What exactly are your talents in this field? Be honest, don't be overly critical of yourself, and consider asking others for their advice and honest opinions. Be willing to accept praise and criticism.

2. How much do you know about the field? You may need to do additional research, and will undoubtedly discover avenues that you had never considered. You may even come up with a completely new approach of your own!

If you do decide to take things further, start modestly and keep your risks to a minimum. If you decide to keep your hobby as just that, then that's fine. But make sure you don't fall into the trap of thinking, "If I enjoy it so much, then I can't do it as a living. My job has to be something that's a bit of a stressful grind; that's what jobs are." The sooner you rid yourself of this idea, the better.

Show your true colors
Even if you decide not to make your hobby a way of life, you may be able to incorporate the special qualities and skills it brings out in you into your everyday job.

"But I Can't Draw!"

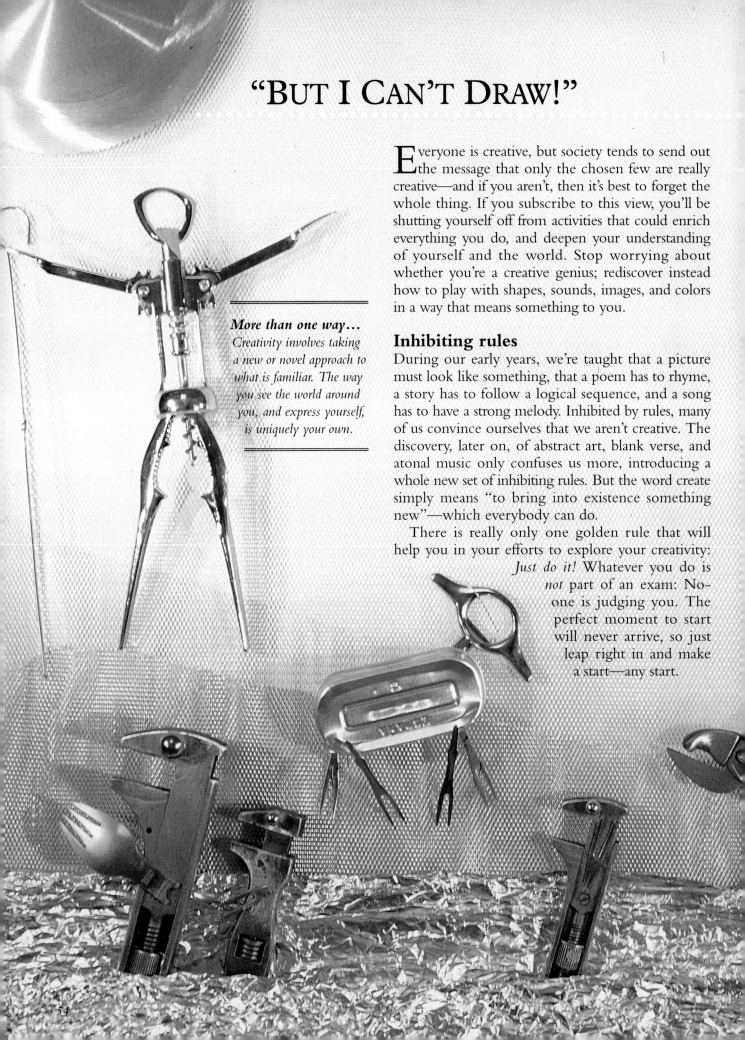

Everyone is creative, but society tends to send out the message that only the chosen few are really creative—and if you aren't, then it's best to forget the whole thing. If you subscribe to this view, you'll be shutting yourself off from activities that could enrich everything you do, and deepen your understanding of yourself and the world. Stop worrying about whether you're a creative genius; rediscover instead how to play with shapes, sounds, images, and colors in a way that means something to you.

Inhibiting rules

During our early years, we're taught that a picture must look like something, that a poem has to rhyme, a story has to follow a logical sequence, and a song has to have a strong melody. Inhibited by rules, many of us convince ourselves that we aren't creative. The discovery, later on, of abstract art, blank verse, and atonal music only confuses us more, introducing a whole new set of inhibiting rules. But the word create simply means "to bring into existence something new"—which everybody can do.

There is really only one golden rule that will help you in your efforts to explore your creativity: *Just do it!* Whatever you do is *not* part of an exam: No-one is judging you. The perfect moment to start will never arrive, so just leap right in and make a start—any start.

More than one way...
Creativity involves taking a new or novel approach to what is familiar. The way you see the world around you, and express yourself, is uniquely your own.

Just write the first thing that comes into your head, make any kind of mark on your drawing paper, sing any sequence of notes. You may feel more relaxed and free if you try this in unexpected places with no fuss or preamble, such as drawing a picture on a paper napkin in a restaurant.

Forget your inhibitions

To be truly creative, you need to put aside your preconceptions and consider the two following points:
1. Creativity is not a question of "divine inspiration" alighting on people out of the blue—a mysterious, exclusive club that you can never join. It is a question of practice, experimentation, playing around with ideas, and of believing that it is important for you to express yourself in these ways.
2. You are responsible for your own creativity, and should never worry about what other people might think of your efforts. Leave them to express themselves in ways that mean something to them—you have your own path to follow.

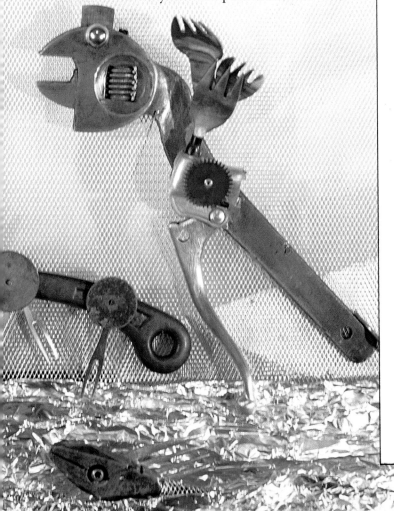

TIME TO PLAY

As part of your daily routine, try increasing the number of creative things you do. Sing or dance along to a tune on the radio; tap out a rhythm using kitchen utensils; make up a story, rather than reading one; start a sketchbook or journal. Once you start to express your creativity, you will be able to think of all kinds of creative games, but here are a few ideas to get you started.

Words
• Make up stories with children or friends. Try taking turns, with each of you adding a sentence.
• Pick words at random from the dictionary and make up a story using all of them—the more unlikely and outlandish, the better.
• Pick a word from the dictionary that none of you knows. One person writes down its definition, the others write down an invented one. Mix them all up, read them out, then vote on the most likely definition.

Images
• Cut out lots of basic shapes—circles, triangles, rectangles—from paper or cardboard, and arrange them to form new shapes and patterns that you find pleasing.
• Draw a picture of your life, your business, or a relationship. It doesn't have to be realistic; it can be symbolic, such as an arrow with a blazing trail to signify a growing business.

Movement and mime
• Try to mime something—an activity or even an elaborate story—to a group of friends, who have to interpret what you're saying. A game of charades can be great fun.
• Get several people to stand in a line. One person should begin a particular movement, such as bending at the knees repeatedly, with an accompanying sound; the next person should then make a different sound and movement, while the first person continues, until the whole line is moving and making different noises. Don't worry about looking foolish!

GET BACK ON COURSE

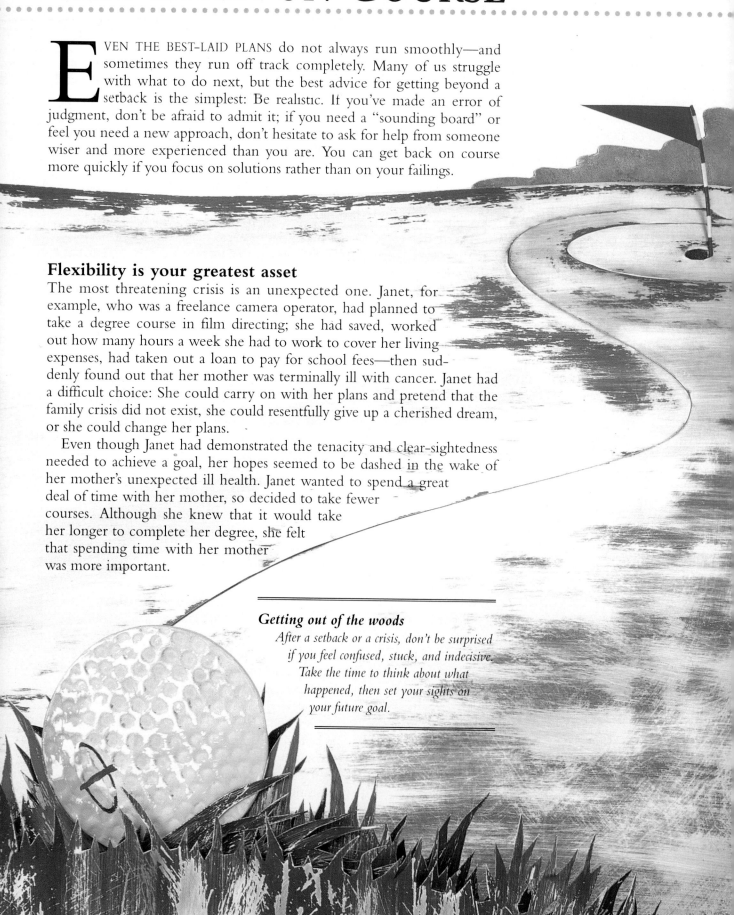

EVEN THE BEST-LAID PLANS do not always run smoothly—and sometimes they run off track completely. Many of us struggle with what to do next, but the best advice for getting beyond a setback is the simplest: Be realistic. If you've made an error of judgment, don't be afraid to admit it; if you need a "sounding board" or feel you need a new approach, don't hesitate to ask for help from someone wiser and more experienced than you are. You can get back on course more quickly if you focus on solutions rather than on your failings.

Flexibility is your greatest asset

The most threatening crisis is an unexpected one. Janet, for example, who was a freelance camera operator, had planned to take a degree course in film directing; she had saved, worked out how many hours a week she had to work to cover her living expenses, had taken out a loan to pay for school fees—then suddenly found out that her mother was terminally ill with cancer. Janet had a difficult choice: She could carry on with her plans and pretend that the family crisis did not exist, she could resentfully give up a cherished dream, or she could change her plans.

Even though Janet had demonstrated the tenacity and clear-sightedness needed to achieve a goal, her hopes seemed to be dashed in the wake of her mother's unexpected ill health. Janet wanted to spend a great deal of time with her mother, so decided to take fewer courses. Although she knew that it would take her longer to complete her degree, she felt that spending time with her mother was more important.

Getting out of the woods
After a setback or a crisis, don't be surprised if you feel confused, stuck, and indecisive. Take the time to think about what happened, then set your sights on your future goal.

During the months before her mother's death, Janet and her sisters spent time going through family photograph albums, and Janet made video tapes of all of them talking to their mother about her life. Janet also kept a journal. Two years after her mother had died, she re-read it and showed it to her sisters, who encouraged her to use it as the basis for a script for her first film—a portrait of a family attempting to cope with illness and bereavement.

Is it your fault?

Sometimes, plans unravel because you haven't calculated the risks properly or heeded early warning signs that things were not going well.

For example, Jane had dated Robert for about two years, and even though she was aware that he was careless with money and seemed to drink too much, she never discussed her feelings with him because she was afraid of appearing too critical. A few months after they married, however, she realized that Robert had a serious problem with alcohol abuse. Trapped in what became an increasingly unhappy relationship, she berated herself for not trusting her instincts and for being "stupid"—which only increased her low self-esteem. Her close friends and family helped her get over this phase of self-blame, and with their encouragement, Jane confronted Robert about his problem.

Learn from your mistakes

Because all of us are human, and will inevitably make mistakes, it helps to remember that what sharpens our judgment, and what makes us more discriminating about people and about appropriate life goals, are the times we "nearly" got it right but didn't. In fact, we often learn most from our deepest disappointments: although they may be hard to bear, they nonetheless provide the chance to look unflinchingly at ourselves, and to discover our strengths and what truly matters to us.

BOUNCING BACK

Resilience in the aftermath of a crisis may be difficult if you blame yourself for it. You may have standards of behavior you feel you've violated—for example, if you've achieved a goal dishonestly—or you may have failed to attain a long-held aspiration. Before you can get going again, you may need to take time to reflect on what went wrong—but without punishing yourself.

Forgive yourself

Feelings of loss or remorse resolve themselves more quickly if they are counterbalanced by positive feelings or insights. While it's important to take responsibility for your behavior, don't get stuck in self-pity or bitter regret. Instead, accept what you have done, but think of yourself as someone who is capable of learning. If you had a child who seriously misbehaved or hurt another person, you would probably reprimand him or her, but would you continue to punish your child every day? It would be far more effective if, as well as repeating the standards you think are important, you provided opportunities for your child to behave better, and acknowledged his or her apologies and attempts to improve.

The fact that you feel regret or remorse over a misguided or insensitive act is a measure of your growth. If you can make amends, do so. If you can't, resolve to act in accord with the goals that will enhance your growth instead of being a cause for regret in the future. If you believe you can do better, you will.

A moment's pause…
Before you spring back into action, you might have to think first about your future direction.

GIVE CHANCE A CHANCE

THE IDEA THAT you should give up trying to control your life might seem a very frightening one. After all, most of us spend our time trying to do the exact opposite, constantly assessing our goals and pursuing them. Although having direction is important, overplanning can be draining: It can take a lot of the joy and spontaneity from life, and may mean that you cannot take up exciting new challenges because they are not planned. Sometimes, simply trusting that life will give you what you need may lead to a more interesting and rewarding existence.

Life is not a machine

Julie, for instance, believed in planning her life and always knew where she wanted to be and what she wanted to be five years ahead. She and her husband had decided when they would start their family, and Julie had decided precisely how she wanted her career to progress—she had plans for almost every waking moment, and nothing in her day was left to chance.

Then, during her late twenties, things started to go wrong. She did not get pregnant and she found it difficult to get promoted at work. Then she discovered her husband was having an affair. Feeling that her life was slipping into chaos, Julie became very depressed and, with the help of her sister, she realized that her exhausting desire to control everything was only contributing to her depression. Her sister, who taught at a school in India, suggested that Julie join her for a long visit. Julie left behind her husband and her job, a spontaneous decision that made her feel happier than she had done for a long time. She viewed the prospect of letting her life take its own course for a while with delight, and resolved to make no plans for a few months, after which she would re-evaluate her goals.

Surprise yourself!
No matter what you do, you can't predict or control everything, so take time out to relax and enjoy life's surprises—some of them might be quite magical and better than anything you planned.

Trying too hard?

Many people find it very difficult to relax and just "see what happens." Some constantly seek to improve themselves and their lives, and adhere rigidly to their plan for achieving their goals, but may not realize that trying very hard to achieve something can often make a task more difficult: You inevitably focus on it more, act from what may be inappropriate expectations, and may be putting undue pressure on yourself and others. For instance, if someone desperately wants a relationship to lead to marriage, he or she may jeopardize what may well be a comfortable and friendly relationship by demanding a commitment too soon, or by appearing desperate and needy. They may not realize that allowing a relationship to grow and develop at its own pace is far more likely to lead to a happy partnership in the long run.

Develop trust

To enhance your enjoyment of life, always leave room for an element of chance, or the opportunity to do something unexpected. The following points will help you think about ways to do this:
• Be spontaneous! Let yourself have a bit of fun by doing something on the spur of the moment.
• Learn to live with not knowing all the answers. As you change and grow, what you want from life will change, and it is impossible to predict what situations you will have to face.
• Realize that you do not need to control everything to survive. If you fear chaos and catastrophe, it may reflect your fear of *inner* chaos and insecurity about your ability to cope with life's vicissitudes.
• Trust that whatever happens in life will aid your growth, and that you either have, or can develop, the qualities needed to cope.

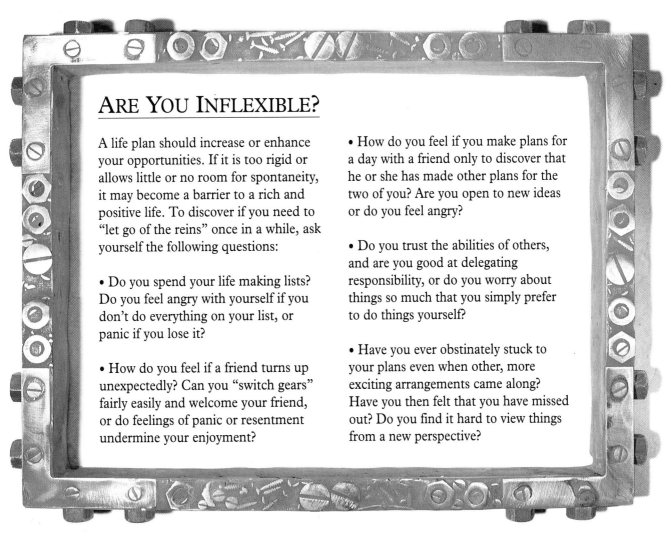

ARE YOU INFLEXIBLE?

A life plan should increase or enhance your opportunities. If it is too rigid or allows little or no room for spontaneity, it may become a barrier to a rich and positive life. To discover if you need to "let go of the reins" once in a while, ask yourself the following questions:

• Do you spend your life making lists? Do you feel angry with yourself if you don't do everything on your list, or panic if you lose it?

• How do you feel if a friend turns up unexpectedly? Can you "switch gears" fairly easily and welcome your friend, or do feelings of panic or resentment undermine your enjoyment?

• How do you feel if you make plans for a day with a friend only to discover that he or she has made other plans for the two of you? Are you open to new ideas or do you feel angry?

• Do you trust the abilities of others, and are you good at delegating responsibility, or do you worry about things so much that you simply prefer to do things yourself?

• Have you ever obstinately stuck to your plans even when other, more exciting arrangements came along? Have you then felt that you have missed out? Do you find it hard to view things from a new perspective?

SPIRITUAL PEACE

ALTHOUGH IT IS A CLICHÉ to say that money can't buy you happiness, it is true that people who have achieved material success still have no guarantee against a sense of emptiness or lack of purpose. Spiritual peace—a sense of inner calm, a deep sense of connection with the world or with "something" larger than yourself, and the knowledge that your life has meaning—is something that many people seek, sometimes without even realizing it.

What is spirituality?

Defining spirituality is no easy matter. For people with a strong religious faith, it is easy: Spirituality involves faith in their god and taking part in specific religious practices. However, spirituality does not need to be connected to organized religion. For those who do not adhere to one particular creed, or indeed who do not believe in a god, getting in touch with the spiritual side of themselves can pose problems. What does spirituality mean to them, and how can they find out more about it?

Most spiritual disciplines see life as a journey toward greater wisdom, joy, and purpose, and urge us to examine our inner life. Time set aside for contemplation, meditation, or prayer is often an important part of the spiritual path—time to discover your thoughts and feelings about what is good and worthwhile or even sacred about your life. Many spiritually inclined yet non-religious people work on being in touch with what they call a "higher self," a part of themselves that might also be called the soul. Other people believe this part of themselves is connected to their god.

Many people express their spirituality by giving time and energy to activities that touch their idealistic, intuitive side—things such as going into the countryside and experiencing its beauty and stillness; listening to soothing music; learning how to meditate; working with like-minded people for a social cause; or reading books that are a source of religious or spiritual thoughts to ponder. Some people feel their creativity serves a higher purpose, which is more important to them than personal recognition. Any of these paths may help you discover yourself and a deeper sense of meaning.

SEEKING ANSWERS

There are a few things you might do in your search for answers about the spiritual life:
• Ensure that you spend time alone, and try not to fill your life with busy-ness as a way to avoid thinking about what may be lacking in your life.
• See yourself as part of a wider community of people to whom you feel you have important responsibilities, and to whom you are connected simply because you are human.
• Try to recognize that the amount of money you have has very little bearing on your ability to feel at peace with yourself.
• Consider exploring your religious beliefs— whether this means returning to the place you worshipped in as a child, or going with different friends to the church or temple they attend.
• Don't consider that finding spiritual peace is something beyond ordinary people. You don't have to be particularly saintly.
• Enjoy your life as it is now, whether or not it is how you would like it. Live each day to the full.

Making changes

Charles and his wife had everything money could buy: a beautiful house, lovely clothes, vacations all over the world. He was not a particularly introspective person, and thought little about meaningful issues. However, one evening in 1985, Charles saw a television program about the famine in Ethiopia. He was so profoundly shocked that he decided to sell his expensive second car and donate the proceeds to the famine appeal. From then on, he gave more of his income to social and charitable causes, feeling that the way to live a moral and peaceful existence was by giving something back to the world.

Not many people want to change their lives in the way that Charles did, and "dropping out" is often not possible or desirable. It's important to be aware, however, whether your life has become too caught up with striving for material things, leaving you little time to consider the direction of your life, or philosophical or spiritual issues.

The journey never ends

Because your spiritual life is a journey, you probably will never achieve complete spiritual fulfillment. In the process of living and growing, circumstances will always challenge you to live by, or to change, what you believe. Spiritual peace is probably something to be aimed for, rather than a goal that can be achieved once and for all. However, many people find that a sense of spirituality or religious faith deeply enriches their lives, and brings them closer to the real meaning and purpose of why we are here. At some point in our lives, most of us choose to walk this enriching path—and discover joy and fulfillment while doing so.

What lights your way?
Making time for calm reflection to understand yourself and your values, and feeling that your life has purpose, will contribute to spiritual peace.

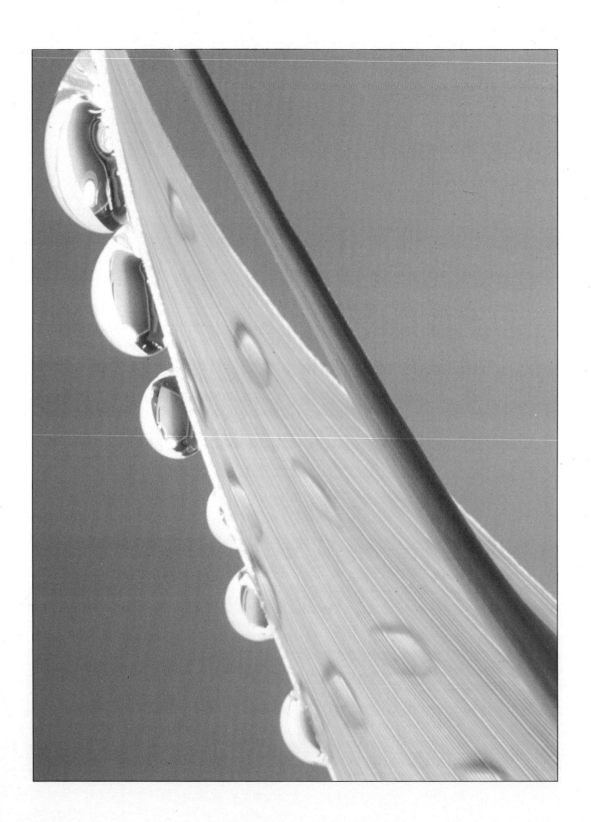

CHAPTER THREE

YOUR OUTER WORLD

THE QUEST FOR PERSONAL GROWTH is to some degree a solitary journey, but it is almost never undergone in isolation. We are individuals, but we also exist in a wider social context, and our relationships with others have an enormous influence and impact on our attitudes, thinking, and behavior throughout our lives.

While it is important to follow the dictates of your heart and your needs, you should also take account of the realities and demands of your outer world. Your relationships and social connections are not only a source of companionship, fun, and stimulation; they can also give you valuable insights into yourself and feedback about how the world perceives you (see "Making Connections," pp. 64-65). Loving, supportive relationships aid mutual growth, while those that are limiting, destructive, or overdependent hinder it. The questionnaire, "Have You Got Room to Grow?" on pages 66-67 will help you understand how your relationships, and your attitudes to them, affect your growth.

Our families form our first experience of the outer world and social interaction, so we learn much of our behavior from them. "The Growing Family," pages 68-69, suggests that open communication—including healthy dissent—makes for strong relationships and a positive outlook on the world. Good communication is the cornerstone of all relationships. If you feel free to express yourself, and can approach your differences with others with clarity and a positive attitude, you can build a bridge over potential discord rather than deepening the divide (see "Good Communication," pp. 74-75.)

Work can be much more than just a way of earning your living. If your work doesn't fulfill you, it helps to identify areas of dissatisfaction so you can consider how to improve them, or perhaps change your career (see "Just the Job?" pp. 78-79, and "Is Your Career on Course?" pp. 80-81). It is also valuable to remember that you are far more than what you do; there are many aspects to your personality, and your identity derives from a whole range of personal qualities, traits, skills, attitudes, and behavior (see "You Are What You Are," pp. 82-83).

If you have been successful in your career, but still feel unfulfilled, you may want to try a new tack—but be wary of changing your lifestyle. "Successful and Stuck?" on pages 84-85 contains inspiring stories of people who have overcome doubt and frustration, and successfully rechanneled their skills.

RESPONDING TO INFLUENCES FROM YOUR OUTER WORLD IN A POSITIVE WAY CAN FOSTER PERSONAL GROWTH, AND CREATE NEW SOURCES OF EMOTIONAL SUSTENANCE AND SUPPORT.

MAKING CONNECTIONS

FROM OUR INFANCY, we gradually learn that other people are essential for our survival, and that relationships—with family members, partners, friends, and work colleagues—are the mainstay of life. As we grow toward adulthood, we find ways to adapt to the needs and expectations of others, while striving to stay in touch with our inner selves. The qualities of your inner life—your feelings, hopes, creative gifts, and spiritual needs—are constantly challenged by the demands of the outside world. Ideally, this interplay between the two can harness your strengths, and enrich both your own life and the lives of those around you.

Inner and outer connections

If you want to have healthy, rewarding relationships with other people, you first need to have a good relationship with yourself. Healthy self-esteem is at the core of happiness and personal growth. You need to love and value yourself for the unique individual you are, rather than measuring your worth by how much you achieve or by the approval of others.

When you are in tune with yourself, when there is a harmonious connection between who you really are and the way you behave and respond to others, you will feel "centered": strong, balanced, inwardly serene, yet full of life and receptive to other people. Strong self-esteem helps you to enjoy closeness and to be enriched by the experience and attitudes of others—without desperately needing them to make you feel whole by filling some gap in yourself.

Reality check

In order for you to grow, your relationship with the outside world must be based on reality. Sometimes, our past experiences leave such an impression on us that we use them as the template for the way we respond in other, superficially similar, situations—regardless of whether or not such behavior is still appropriate or likely to make us happier or more fulfilled. Remember this advice: "Trust the territory, not the map"—in other words, take your cue from the reality of a situation rather than from your inner perception of that situation and what has gone

A constant interplay
Our feelings and perceptions are continually challenged and revitalized by the demands of the outside world.

home truth: that her behavior with men was often abrasive and rejecting. Karen realized that she approached new relationships with the expectation that men would find her boring, and so she acted defensively. The next time a man flirted with her, she tried to respond in a more relaxed way, and to observe his reaction. She noticed that he was by no means yawning or making excuses to walk away— and this made her feel more confident about talking with him and then going out with him.

Learn from others

Other people are the most helpful guides you have when it comes to comparing your assumptions and feelings with reality. Take note of the feedback you receive, especially if you keep getting the same responses. Be aware of how others respond to you, and observe how their behavior and reactions compare with your own. We can all learn from each other: Look for good role models, ask wise friends how they would act in certain situations, question your opinions and beliefs by talking with people who are very different from you. Let others bring fresh air into your life, challenge your assumptions, and keep you alive to new and different possibilities.

A healthy balance

Emotional maturity partly depends on an ability to reconcile your own needs with the challenges of the outer world. Reality will necessitate modifying your ideas and plans at times, but negotiating these compromises, adjustments, and changes is not something from which you should shrink. The way we learn to be flexible, and to adapt to changing circumstances, is part of the process of personal growth. The capacity to use your connections with other people to inform your judgment and approach to life increases your potential to change and develop.

before. Essentially, this means keeping a flexible outlook by giving up your preconceptions and adjusting when you need to.

For example, Karen was beginning to think that there was something wrong with her when she found herself, at 37, embarking on another year without a partner. Eventually, a friend told her a

Reconciling needs
Being "in synch" with your inner needs and taking account of the demands of your outer world will help you form better relationships with others—and with yourself.

Have You Got Room to Grow?

Personal growth can be enhanced if you have supportive people around you; on the other hand, it can also be hindered if, for example, you are over-dependent on others, if you keep people at a distance, or if those around you are afraid or resentful of your changes. To find out how your relationships affect your growth, read the following statements and tick the ones that apply to you.

Section 1

• It's important to me to feel as though I can make people feel happy and content.
• I find it difficult to express my thoughts and feelings openly.
• I often end up doing what others want to do.
• I don't feel that people really know me, even those I'm closest to.
• If people really knew me, they probably wouldn't like me.
• I often feel I'm being what people expect me to be; sometimes, I end up feeling frustrated and even resentful.
• I'm most comfortable when I'm alone.
• I don't generally turn to others for help or comfort, but rely on myself instead.
• People often share their problems with me.
• I find it difficult to express physical affection.
• I sometimes worry that I've said or done something to offend or anger someone.
• I'd like to feel more comfortable with people than I do at present.

Section 2

• I'm not afraid to speak my mind, no matter whom I'm with.
• I tend to argue frequently with people—strangers as well as family.
• I'm sometimes puzzled that I seem to hurt, offend, or frighten people.
• When I'm annoyed or angry, everyone knows it.
• I sometimes provoke others to get angry or argue with me.
• I feel that people don't really know me.
• I find it difficult to show feelings like love, affection, and sadness.
• I feel people expect me to be tough and strong.
• My best friends tend to be more sensitive or compliant than I am; sometimes, I think they're weaker than I am.
• People need me more than I need them.
• In my close relationships, I always feel I'm the strong one, and am expected to "lead."
• There are times when I'd like to be able to lean on someone, and show my vulnerable side.

Securely attached

Psychologists know that the more a child feels there is a solid base from which to explore, the more likely he or she will be to face the world feeling secure. This is largely determined by the parents' own attitude: If they believe that growth, independence, and curiosity are positive qualities, and are confident about facing the challenges of the outside world, the children will feel the same. Parents who are afraid of the world will pass this fear on to their children.

Lesley's mother, for example, had worried constantly over her daughter's health and safety; she overdressed, overfed, and generally overprotected Lesley from what she viewed as a frightening world. In turn, Lesley became an anxious and timid adult. When her own daughter became a rebellious teenager, Lesley was surprised to find that she felt relieved that her daughter was able to break free and assert herself—something that she had never been able to do with her own mother.

Happy family conflict

Although most people dread conflict, it is a normal, natural, and inevitable part of family life, an environment in which each member is constantly changing and growing. What undermines many families is not conflict but lack of communication, and problems tend to begin with the parents: If they talk openly and honestly with each other, the children will follow their lead. A family that can freely discuss its

Airing your views
Family members should be encouraged to express their views honestly and openly—but without ridiculing others.

problems, even if this leads to loud, disruptive arguments, is much more likely to stick together than one that refuses to acknowledge difficulties. Only if conflict is the sole way of interacting is it a serious threat to a family; most families, however, swing between periods of conflict and contentment.

As you change, you may find that some family members will be supportive, while others may feel threatened by your new attitudes or behavior, and be dismissive, hostile, or rejecting. Many people find change makes them feel insecure, and worry that their relationship with you may also change, so sensitive and continuous communication is essential.

GET TALKING

If you feel your family does not communicate, try the following suggestions. They may be difficult to instigate, but if you keep trying, they may prove to be the answer to many family problems.
- **Arrange regular family meetings.** Everyone should attend. Let each person speak for a full five minutes, without criticism or interruption, about anything he or she feels affects them or family life in general. Then each person comments in turn. Don't enforce any rules other than these; simply allow people to speak their minds.

Although these meetings may feel artificial, they lead to greater freedom of expression and trust. If family members don't show up, have the meeting anyway; they'll probably be too curious to stay away for long.
- **Spend time with each family member.** Make time to do this at least once a week, and ensure that it is completely confidential. As in the family meeting, allow the person to speak openly and honestly. Encourage him or her to ask questions or express feelings that might be difficult, or simply to share private, enjoyable stories.

PRIVATE SELF, PUBLIC SELF

We begin life not knowing what it means to be embarrassed. We laugh, cry, and scream openly, and reveal our most intimate physical functions without shame or self-consciousness. Gradually, however, we become aware of what we should and shouldn't do: Along with learning that we mustn't eat with our mouth open, or slouch at the table, we learn that it is better not to show certain feelings in public. Although it's quite healthy and normal to have both a private and a public self, the separation between the two should not be a such a great divide that you often feel you have a "false" self and a "true" self; instead, the ideal situation is a natural continuum that reflects the varying and appropriate degrees of intimacy and trust you have with those around you; you should also feel that you can be flexible.

Sometimes, our negative feelings, such as our fears and anxieties, or modes of behavior that we've been taught are "bad" and unacceptable, become deeply buried within us; frequently, such feelings are beyond our conscious awareness except when we're caught off guard— and especially during times of stress or crisis. Our temporary glimpses of these hidden feelings, however, while sometimes frightening, are windows through which we can discover our deeper selves.

What happens, however, if you feel that your real self is locked away most of the time, that you never feel able to be who you really are? It may lead you to feel that you can't really trust anyone, and won't ever be able to share your deeper emotions. Indeed, the façade, or false self, that you present to the world may be so far removed from your true self that you may not even be aware of this.

Layers of identity
In public, many of us have a more limited range of responses, or more formal behavior. In private, we're usually more spontaneous.

You may only be conscious of the fact that you often feel isolated and lonely even when surrounded by "close" friends or family. Some people, however, have a different problem, in which they find it hard to separate their public and private selves; for example, an actor may always play to an audience, seeking to be the center of everyone's attention, even in the company of good friends with whom he or she might be expected to "drop the mask." Similarly, a politician or other public figure may become so used to presenting a front that it can be hard to let it go.

When the public self takes over, the private self may get lost. In the short term, a person who over-identifies with a public role may seem fine, and other people may not notice anything wrong; in the long term, however, this loss of an authentic self often leads to unhappiness and lack of fulfillment. There may be depression, a sense of emptiness, a hollowness in relationships, and a feeling of drifting through life without purpose. Some people turn to food, drugs, or other destructive ways of expressing their lack of fulfillment—but never get to the bottom of their problems.

Respecting privacy

People who don't keep their public and private selves separate may be unable to respect their own or others' need for privacy, and so may be as lonely as those who always hide their real selves. We've all encountered people who readily confide in everyone, even strangers, telling us their life story and personal problems when we've only just met. It makes us uncomfortable because we sense that it is inappropriate; there has been no gradual build-up of trust, no legacy of shared experiences that contribute to mutually acceptable boundaries. As a listener, you may end up feeling anonymous—as though you could be anybody—because the person who is unburdening him- or herself may not give you the chance to reveal yourself at all. This kind of behavior often stems from a desperate need to be close to others coupled with a terrifying and often unconscious fear of real intimacy, and such people may seem to have many "close" friends yet remain isolated and lonely.

REVEALING YOURSELF

Although you might find it hard to trust others, taking the risk and letting people get to know you has tremendous benefits. Your friends, partner, and other people can actually help you to stay in touch with your true self. One of the greatest joys of healthy relationships is the feeling that you are loved and accepted for who you really are. Being able to relax completely in the company of others allows you to express yourself freely, and to let your private self come to the fore.

Friends can also help you discover what you cannot see easily in yourself. Given the opportunity and encouraged to be candid, most friends will tell you honestly and kindly what you want to know about yourself. Bear in mind, of course, that each person's view will be based on their own needs and expectations, so do ask more than one person. You may find that certain friends do not take you seriously, or will feel too awkward about being so honest. Accept that such openness is not easy for many people, and be patient or talk with another friend. Whatever you do, you will undoubtedly benefit from opening up to others.

Mutual openness and growth

Many of us fear that open communication will not be based on love, honesty, and respect, and thus find it hard to build trusting relationships. But having at least one person that you can say anything to, who accepts you as you really are, and who is honest if you ask for his or her opinion is invaluable. Not only is learning to be open in this way essential to personal growth, but such a relationship also benefits *both* of you. You'll be strengthened by each other's affection and concern for your mutual welfare, and by sharing your secret fears, you can help each other find ways to cope with difficulties, and to overcome obstacles to self-fulfillment.

GROWING TOGETHER

The intimacy of a long-term, committed relationship is, at its best, an ideal context for the personal growth and development of both partners. Such a relationship makes you feel loved and accepted, and provides a stable base from which you can expand your horizons and fulfill yourself in the outside world. If you feel secure in each other's love, the prospect of one or both of you changing and working on personal growth will not be seen as a threat but as something that can bring more happiness and vitality to the partnership as well as the individual. A partner provides love, emotional support, and encouragement, but it is also helpful if he or she has some understanding of and is sympathetic to your inner life, and your emotional history and patterns.

You and your mirror

Studies of couples demonstrate that we have an uncanny knack of choosing partners who, although they may come from different backgrounds, have similar or complementary problems and anxieties. This is often part of what makes two people feel comfortable with each other. For example, two partners may both have low self-esteem and "recognize" the familiar attitudes and behavior, although in some cases, such mirroring is distorted: for instance, an abusive, domineering man and a submissive, unassertive woman may be attracted to each other, often because this bully-victim pairing echoes a formative experience for each of them in some way.

On the other hand, what may look to outsiders as the attraction of opposites is, in fact, a bond—not necessarily an unhealthy one—formed by complementary emotional patterns.

Wedlock deadlock
There may be times in a relationship when one or both partners feel frustrated, or that they want to move in different directions.

MENDING THE PAST

Being part of a committed couple not only serves to help you and your partner look to the future, but also provides a way to mend past hurts. Although we may joke about the man who wants to be mothered by his wife, or the 30-year-old "daddy's girl," such relationships are not necessarily examples of stunted development; instead, they may indicate that within the adult bond between the couple there is also room to express an earlier stage of the personality.

When two people sometimes allow each other the freedom to behave like wild adolescents, playful children, or lovers in the first throes of romance, it provides the chance to express their younger, more

Echoes of the past
The qualities of our parents—both positive and negative—inevitably shape our choice of partner.

exuberant selves. More importantly, it demonstrates great trust and mutual acceptance: Past grief, regrets, and failures may be revealed and accepted—perhaps for the first time. It's not uncommon for people to choose a partner who resembles a parent, even a difficult or abusive one, in an unconscious attempt to re-create old conflicts—but it's also an attempt to *heal* them by seeking better resolutions.

Many couples find that their relationship atrophies because they believe that there is no room for their younger, more vulnerable self. Remaining open to another's past is part of caring about him or her. In return, you too may feel loved and accepted for who you really are.

For example, Mary, who was timid and dependent, was attracted to John's independence. In turn, John recognized that he could be aloof, and felt comfortable with Mary's sincerity and gentleness. Both had difficulty expressing their emotional needs, but their relationship was successful and emotionally healthy due to the fact that, despite their ostensible differences, each was *willing* to learn from the other.

In problematic relationships, however, there may be little willingness to compromise, or to recognize that one partner's qualities either mirror the other's, or compensate for their lack of those traits. If both partners are resistant to change, or simply too anxious to recognize the need for it, they may remain stuck in a pattern that holds both of them back. Conversely, in good relationships that are psychologically healthy, partners are able to talk freely and openly with each other and discuss difficulties and areas they'd like to change. Provided that the intention is sincere and meant to encourage mutual growth—rather than to coerce one partner to conform to the

other's expectations—such communication usually results in deeper trust, respect, and intimacy, and prevents problems from becoming insoluble.

Facing change

As we enter a new phase of life, new roles must be found so that we relate to one another in a way that furthers, rather than inhibits, both our own and our partner's growth. Marriages often fail because one partner no longer wishes to be frustrated or held back from broadening his or her experience and development, while the other is unwilling to tackle change, perhaps fearing that he or she might be less valuable or needed. In these situations, couples may drift apart, become engaged in intense conflict, or feel a sense of futility as they reluctantly recognize that their marriage is no longer a source of happiness and fulfillment.

If this passage is negotiated with insight and empathy for each other's fears and anxieties, however, the relationship can move from strength to strength. Because they have a history, couples often have to undergo a painful process of re-evaluation and mourning as the old order is left behind, but mutual support can lead to the creation of a different but rewarding future—one that benefits both of you.

GOOD COMMUNICATION

Although we may realize that communication costs nothing, and we may love talking to our partner or friends, we all have times when we find it difficult, or impossible, to say something important to someone close to us—particularly if we feel the other person may not want to hear it. It sometimes seems easier to say nothing instead, but you risk tolerating a state of uneasy truce that passes for peace instead of resolving an issue that may cause tension, frustration, or resentment.

In all close relationships, there are a few things that are best left unsaid, but unless people feel free to express themselves, the relationship may stagnate and founder. It's not easy to tell someone you care for that he or she has hurt or disappointed you—but it's also important to understand the difference between selfishly expressing your negative feelings with little regard for another's response, and attempting to discuss difficult issues that affect you both.

Finding a way to communicate

You can make a vital contribution to effective communication by aiming for clarity and openness, and by trying to be less defensive; you can also help your partner to do the same. Two people in an intimate relationship—whether partners, friends, or relatives—know how to tap into each other's vulnerabilities like no-one else does. The potential to hurt each other is therefore enormous, and it is up to you both not to be reckless or to exploit this.

If you tend to regard each discussion as a potential battle, and approach it as an opportunity to blame or punish the other person, or the chance to enact a long-wished-for revenge, you might well score a short-term victory—but it could damage or even end the relationship. Also bear in mind that if you expect to be attacked, and act in a defensive or hostile way, your attitude may prompt your partner to be more critical than he or she would be if you appeared willing to hear what needed to be aired. A more positive approach is to realize that you are both affected by your problem, and are trying to find an outcome that will be better for each of you as individuals—and both of you as a couple.

Bridging the gulf

It's important to accept that you might not like what you hear, but keep an open mind and be prepared to learn from the other person and deepen your self-understanding. Good relationships are built up over time, and are made stronger through empathy and commitment. Intimacy is something you work toward. No matter how close you are, it is unrealistic to expect perfect agreement and understanding at all times. Even if you manage to say what you mean, you won't necessarily get what you want. Simply by trying to communicate better, however, you will at least build a bridge between you rather than widen the gulf.

POSITIVE TALK

Good communication is the keystone of happy relationships that foster mutual development. Use the following guidelines to help you communicate with greater confidence and effectiveness.

1. Be attentive, and focus on the present issue.
• Don't walk away or change the subject.
• Don't recount past hurts and disasters.
• Avoid using the words "always" or "never."
• Don't say "no" when you mean "yes," or vice versa.

2. Take responsibility for yourself.
• Don't expect the other person to know what you want, feel, or need unless you tell him or her.
• Turn all complaints and criticisms into requests. Rather than complaining that someone isn't doing what you would prefer, ask them if they will do it.

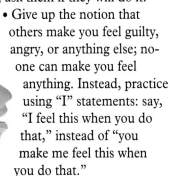

• Give up the notion that others make you feel guilty, angry, or anything else; no-one can make you feel anything. Instead, practice using "I" statements: say, "I feel this when you do that," instead of "you make me feel this when you do that."

3. Allow others to accept responsibility.
• Listen carefully to what others have to say. Don't assume you know what they think or feel.
• Be sure you have really understood what the other person has said. Check this by reiterating their statements as questions: "Do you mean…?"
• Stop yourself when you begin to finish the other person's sentences, or think or feel for them.
• Unless you are absolutely sure what the other person means, needs, or wants, always *ask*.

4. Don't defend yourself from criticism.
• Don't defend yourself by pointing out how the other person is guilty of the same offense.
• Get used to the idea that you're both imperfect, but that it doesn't devalue either of you.
• Acknowledge when the other person has said something that might have a grain of truth to it— even if you don't like what you hear.
• Avoid blunt denials or excuses; instead, use expressions such as, "I see your point" or "I didn't realize you felt that way."

GIVING AND GETTING

IVING TO OTHERS can be a way to explore new avenues of personal growth. All of us, no matter what our situation in life, have a contribution to make, from the simple "give and take" of everyday life, such as the adjustments and compromises we make to maintain a harmonious family life or good atmosphere at work, to feeling and acting on a deep concern for the welfare of other people—some of whom we may not personally know.

Can you give something up?

Anyone who is serious about personal growth or achieving a dream discovers that some kind of sacrifice is often an integral part of following that commitment. Whatever your aim, whatever the area you want to grow in, ask yourself what you arc prepared to give up in order to achieve greater benefit or reward.

For example, imagine you have a demanding job, but want a degree in business administration to enhance your future prospects. After finding an evening program that takes three years to complete, you would need to ask yourself questions, such as: Am I willing to give up holidays in order to have time to study for exams or write essays? Can I cut down on expenditures to pay the tuition fees? Will I miss the time I now spend with friends and family, and could I carry on without their enthusiastic support? Asking yourself realistic questions about what you're willing to give up in order to reach a specific goal will help to determine how motivated you are; motivation is an essential first step toward achieving personal growth.

Mutual benefit
Giving not only benefits the recipient; it also can be psychologically liberating for the person who gives because it makes room for new interests or growth.

APPROPRIATE GIVING

If you tend to put the goals, needs, and wishes of others before your own, it may be the reason why your personal growth has been erratic or blocked. In his book, *10 Steps to Positive Living*, Dr. Windy Dryden suggests the following points to help keep you on track:

1. Strive to be authentic.
Be honest about your wants and needs, and don't fall into the trap of becoming a martyr.

2. Honor your commitments to yourself.
If something is important to you, don't vacillate or be persuaded that it is not important.

3. Act from enlightened self-interest.
Look after your own interests, but remain flexible when dealing with the needs and interests of others. Don't discount what *you* want, or assume that your opinion is less important than what others think.

Are you feeling guilty?

If other people try to manipulate you to "give" them something—such as support, money, or respect—and accuse you of being "selfish" if you're unwilling, you should question their motives as well as your own. Dr. Dryden suggests that you don't have to feel guilty if a so-called generous action would threaten your "safety, well-being, comfort, or view of yourself." Remember that, while others have the right to make a request, they do not have the right to force you to act in a particular way. You always have the right to say no.

Have you given too much?
It's very easy to expend too much of your energy giving to others, but you may have nothing left for yourself.

Can you give something back?

Many people gain great personal satisfaction and fulfillment through giving to others. They may even be drawn to one of the so-called helping or caring professions, such as teaching or social work. Many others undertake voluntary work, such as fund-raising for a favorite charity.

The motives behind selfless behavior vary from person to person. Perhaps you have been raised in an environment in which courtesy and respect were important. Developmental psychologists believe that infants and children have little sense of an isolated self, and because they have no "ego structure," they have an inbuilt empathy for others; this is why a young child may become upset in the presence of another injured, crying child. Research has also suggested that if children are treated with consistent affection and consideration, and their feelings taken seriously, their capacity for empathy persists: They can imagine how others feel and identify with them by recalling their own feelings.

Giving and growing

As an adult, you may consciously formulate a personal morality, the values and standards of behavior that you support and try to live by. For some people, their expression of love and responsibility goes beyond their immediate friends and family, and encompasses a wider community. Why do they do this? Usually, because they feel they wish to contribute to the well-being and security of others, or perhaps to express their gratitude for being helped themselves. Many people whose lives have been changed by one particular teacher may find that they want to teach themselves, to inspire others in the way they were inspired.

Giving may also be prompted by reparation: the need to "make good," or to restore what has been lost. People who have suffered in some way often share the strength they have gained through loss, sometimes by starting a support group, or sometimes by being a wise and trusted friend who offers help when needed. For example, people who have known bereavement are usually the most comforting companions when someone is feeling the shock of grief for the first time.

Whatever your motives, giving always provides the opportunity to extend yourself beyond the boundaries of who you think you are. When you get involved with anything outside yourself, your feelings about your identity may be challenged and stretched, but your self-understanding—and very often your relationships—will almost invariably deepen. Far from feeling depleted by your generosity, you will often discover that you're actually a "bigger" person than you think you are.

JUST THE JOB?

Appreciate the benefits
When a job you are committed to and usually enjoy feels frustrating, look for the positive points.

I S YOUR WORK FULFILLING? Or is it just a means of earning a living? The idea of enjoying what you do might seem like an unattainable dream because, for many people, work is seen as a necessary evil. However, if you are in work, you may spend half your waking hours or more at your job, so it makes sense to do everything in your power to ensure that it is a source of satisfaction rather than frustration. You don't have to have the perfect job or a sense of vocation to find your work fulfilling. Knowing what's important to you, and adopting a positive attitude, will help you make the most of your career—allowing you to gain maximum value from your job's plus points without becoming too frustrated by the minuses.

A job or a career?
Most people want work to be interesting and financially rewarding, but usually have to compromise according to what is most important. Striking a balance between fulfillment and money can be difficult, however. People whose work is their vocation, such as some writers, artists, and musicians, those who follow a spiritual life, or who work in the caring professions or for charities often feel it is more important to pursue their calling than to earn a great

deal of money, although they may also use their talents in more commercial ways: An artist might teach art, for example, or a doctor helping refugees might take on higher-paid shifts elsewhere.

For most of us, money is essential, but it doesn't have to be our only reason to work. Studies show that most people would still want to work even if they won a large sum of money, so it seems that work provides much more than a wage. Consider the other benefits you derive from work; are there areas where you could gain greater satisfaction?

• **Camaraderie and friendship:** Work can be an important part of our social network, giving us daily contact with other people, some of whom may become good friends. Could you organize social activities, sports teams, or get-togethers?

• **Sense of achievement:** Completing a project or task can be very satisfying. Could you be more focused about finishing off things, or set yourself higher standards for the work you do?

• **Challenge:** Stretching your capabilities, skills, and the boundaries of what you feel comfortable with increases your confidence and self-esteem. Could you ask to take on a challenging task, have more training, or extend your responsibilities?

• **Using your talents:** Making good use of your qualities and experience is what helps make work fulfilling. Is there more potential in your job for you to use your abilities?

Change how you see it

As in other areas of life, attitude is all-important. Your job may be boring, and not what you actively set out to do, but you can still make the most of it. Focus on the positive aspects, give it your commitment, and take pride in carrying out even minor tasks efficiently and to a high standard. If morale is low among your colleagues, try organizing out-of-work activities for you all to help foster a better team spirit and a more positive atmosphere.

Try to view your job in a way that helps you make the most of it—and of yourself. For example, if you feel overqualified for your work, and frustrated by a lack of challenge or advancement, don't just moan about it; decide that you can do it really well, and come up with ideas about how it could be done better; this will help you make your mark and increase your sense of satisfaction.

PREPARE FOR CHANGE

Even if you've always been happy in your work, you may still want a change: Perhaps you've outgrown your job and need a fresh challenge in a similar field, or you want to venture into pastures new? If you are considering a change of career, bear the following points in mind:
• Ask yourself what you really want to do. Many people reject their dreams as unrealistic without even trying to see if they could attain them.
• Investigate the kind of work you want to do. What qualifications and skills do you need? Could you acquire them? How could you make yourself a better catch to a prospective employer?
• If you don't know what you want to do—but know it's not what you're doing now—consider career counseling. This can help you decide which jobs would suit your personality and skills.
• Look at books aimed at people planning a career change, such as the annually updated *What Color Is Your Parachute?* by **Richard Nelson Bolles.** These can suggest new ideas, as well as practical strategies for making a radical change.

A new beginning
Many people find fulfillment and a fresh start by taking their career in an entirely new direction.

IS YOUR CAREER ON COURSE?

Are you reasonably contented at work, but feel that you're not being stimulated or challenged in any way? Or maybe you've outgrown a career you once enjoyed? If you're not getting all that you could from your working life, you have to know what you need from your job. This questionnaire will help you identify areas where you may feel unfulfilled, and discover what you need in order to develop in your working life.

In the boxes on the right are important factors that can contribute to job satisfaction. Read the questions, which will help you determine how you feel, then write down a number from one to six to rate your current job (1 for a low value or negative response, 6 for a high value or positive response). Then, underneath this figure, write down the number that represents the rating of your ideal job.

Are you satisfied?

Unless you are blissfully happy in your work, there may well be some discrepancies between the two sets of figures. For example, for your ideal job you might rate Skills as 6, yet you rate your current job as only 2 because you have little chance to do what you do best, or no opportunity to learn new skills.

How this works in practice can be seen in the case of Marie, a teacher. Her ideal ratings were: Social 4, Skills 6, Progression 4, Personal 5, Status 4, Money 3, Creativity 3, Authority 2. In her current job, she scored the same for Social, Status, Money, and Creativity. She rated it only 3 for Skills, however, and one point less in both the Personal and Progression categories. She also felt she had too much Authority—a rating of 4, as against her ideal value of 2. As a result of this exercise, Marie decided that, although she did not want to leave teaching, she needed a post that would make more use of her specific subject skills, and that would require her to deputize for the department head less often.

Social. Do you meet many people through your work? Are the people you see on a daily basis pleasant and friendly? Does your work lead to genuine friendships?

Skills. Do you have the chance to do the things you are good at? Are there chances for you to develop the skills and talents that you already have? Does your work provide opportunities for you to acquire new skills?

Status. Does the work offer you the kind of recognition you find meaningful? Are you respected or accepted by your peers, or by the wider society, for what you do?

Personal. Do you enjoy your job? Does it offer you the chance to grow and develop your potential? Are there further challenges for you to look forward to?

Progression. Are there opportunities for promotion? Can you see which positions you might aim for in the future? Do you have a chance to get there? Do you get encouraging feedback from your boss about your prospects?

Money. Are you paid satisfactorily for the work you do? Should you be paid substantially more? Would you do the same job for less money?

Authority. Do you have influence or authority over others? Are you in charge of a team of people? Are your opinions listened to and taken seriously? Do you initiate your own work and plan how you work?

Creativity. Do you have the opportunity to make use of your creative abilities? Do you have to find creative or unconventional solutions to problems?

Your next steps

Now that you know what you like about your job, as well as what needs to be worked on, you can begin to initiate changes. For example, you may be unhappy about working alone too much, and want more contact with other people. Maybe you need to get together with others who work in similar jobs to provide mutual support. Alternatively, you may decide to carry on working alone, but to improve your social life outside of work, perhaps by joining clubs or taking classes.

MOVING FORWARD

If you're discontented with your work, you're not alone. Surveys reveal that about four out of five people are unhappy with important aspects of their jobs. In *What Color Is Your Parachute?*, author Richard Nelson Bolles maintains that the most intelligent—and most rewarding—career choices are also the most informed, where you understand yourself and your needs.

To this end, Bolles suggests that, before you start looking for a new job, you should ask yourself these three important questions about what you want from your work:

1. What are the skills you most enjoy using? Put them in order of importance according to how much you enjoy using them.

2. Where do you want to use them? What are your preferred working conditions, and what kind of people or things do you want to be involved with?

3. What kind of jobs would enable you to use these qualities? Contact relevant organizations, interview people in similar jobs, as well as those who may be able to help you, and read relevant publications, such as specialist trade papers.

YOU ARE WHAT YOU ARE

I F YOU ASK YOURSELF the question "Who am I?" do you tend to describe yourself in terms of your job? Many of us identify so completely with our work that we may derive our sense of identity and self-worth almost entirely from what we *do*, rather than from who we *are*. Having too close a connection between your work and how you feel about yourself can be limiting, however. If your identity is overdependent on what you do for a living, you are not acknowledging the multifaceted person you are. You may also find it frustrating if other people have preconceptions about you, based on their assumptions about the kind of work you do.

Are you only your job?

The question "What do you do?" is probably the one we ask almost automatically when we meet new people. In order for us to "place" people in context, we feel we have to know what they do for a living, and this influences how we behave toward them, even though we may not be conscious of it. For example, we would probably respond differently to a tax inspector or a dentist from the way we might to a hairdresser or an actor; in the first instances, we tend to be slightly anxious and more guarded in our responses, while in the second we might be open, curious, and receptive. We also tend to treat people of higher status differently from those in subordinate positions.

Considering your identity without taking your job as a starting point can be difficult. People tend to look *outside* themselves—at their job and their relationships—rather than inside at their values or at what things are a source of meaning or joy. As a result, your sense of identity may be based on how others see you to the extent that, although you may feel good about yourself as long as people perceive you as successful, if you are perceived to be unsuccessful—if you suddenly become unemployed, for example—you might suffer feelings of inadequacy, profound loss of identity, or worthlessness.

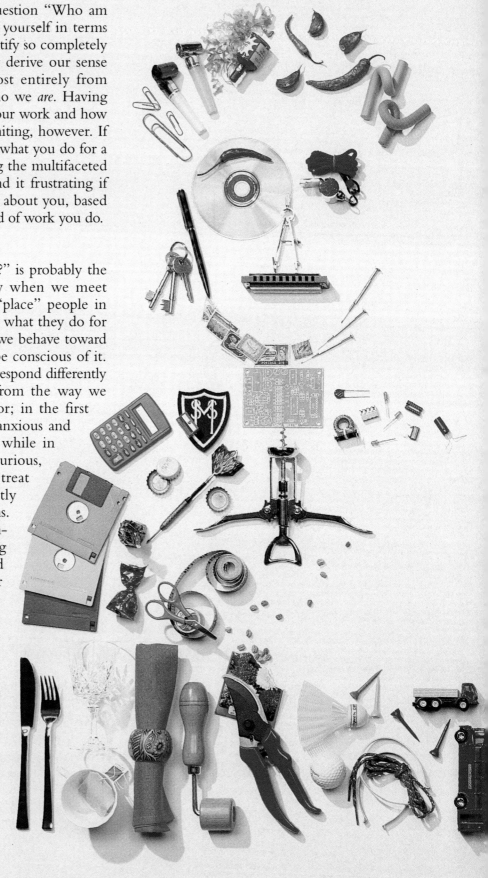

FIND THE REAL YOU

There is nothing wrong with deriving part of your identity from your work; it probably provides you the opportunities to achieve things that are important to you, or the chance to make your mark on the world. But your self-worth is based on more than professional achievements. In the long run, your self-esteem will be higher when you have a balanced and integrated view of who you are, based not only on what you have done at work, but also on the qualities and skills you possess. You can begin to change the way you see yourself by trying the following exercises:

1. Answer the question "What do you do?" without including work. How do you spend your leisure time? What are your interests and hobbies? What causes are you involved with?

2. If you did not have a job, how would you define yourself? Father? Keen cyclist? Amateur painter? Committed environmentalist? Jot down all your other identities; note, too, if you have a preference for any of them, either a favorite interest or the way you would most want to be described to others.

3. List all the things that you are proud of, which do not involve paid work. Consider what they say about you as a person.

4. Make another list of the things you have done outside of earning a living. How do you feel about them? Do you consider them more or less valuable than the work you do now?

5. The next time you meet someone new, practice asking them questions about themselves that do not involve what they do for a living. This may be hard to begin with, but it gets easier with practice.

Sum of many different parts
Qualities such as your integrity,
your capacity for different kinds of
relationships, and the creative skills
that you express in hobbies all
reflect who you are as much—if not
more—than your professional title.

Doors in and out of work

Use the following prompting questions to help you discover and understand your attitudes to work.

• Why do you do what you do? Did you actively choose to do it, or did you simply drift into it?

• What influence did your parents or teachers have on your choice of work?

• If you attended college or university, was this because you were expected to, or you thought it might lead to a good job, or because you thought you would find it interesting and enjoyable?

• What other significant influences—either events or individuals—directed your career choice?

• Were you aware of the problems of your chosen career, or were your expectations unrealistic?

You may realize that you have never really followed your own inclination, but gone along with other people's expectations. Do you perhaps feel worthy only when you achieve something at work or are very productive? Developing your identity outside work, by exploring new interests, looking for ways to use and expand your talents, and trying new experiences and challenges to broaden your horizons, will give your self-esteem and sense of who you are a stronger foundation—and will thus maximize your possibilities for growth.

SUCCESSFUL AND STUCK?

While successful people are often envied by others, success itself carries no automatic guarantee of happiness or fulfillment. Indeed, some people feel almost imprisoned by their success. Perhaps they feel that they didn't really choose to pursue their career in the first place, that they simply fell into it by chance, or succumbed to outside pressure. They may want to change direction completely to stretch themselves further or explore other aspects of their personality and talents, but feel trapped by their obligations and lifestyle into staying in the same field.

What may seem like success to one person will not necessarily feel that way to another. We all have to work out for ourselves what success and achievement mean to us. The following case histories show how people who seemed highly successful to others had to make changes in their lives in order to feel successful themselves. Their stories may prompt you to think about your own life, and about whether it may be time for you to seek out new challenges or to change direction.

Forging a new path

In William's family, it had always been assumed that he would go into his father's law business, even though he had never really wanted to, and deep down felt that he was drawn to a career in the caring professions. When he left school, William studied law at university and obtained a degree, then entered the family firm, taking on more and more work and becoming more experienced until, on his father's retirement, he took over as head of the business—as everyone had expected him to do.

At 40, William became increasingly depressed. He knew he wasn't really suited to his work, and felt unfulfilled and frustrated, but he also knew that he needed the money it provided, and was afraid of disappointing his family. He decided to have extensive career counseling and sought financial advice. This helped him decide that he would maintain ownership of the law firm, but employ other lawyers to take over his work. He could then go back to college to start training for his new chosen career as a psychiatric social worker.

Lonely at the top?
You may have achieved all that you had set your sights on, but then discover that you don't really enjoy your position or responsibilities. Take the time to reconsider your priorities.

A changed outlook

Maureen had always been an academic high-flyer. She had won scholarships at university and, when she sailed into a prestigious scientific research job, she thought little of it. After only five years, she was the first woman ever to have headed a project in her specialist field. She did not value her success, however, and felt it had been comparatively effortless. At only 30, unsure of what her next career move should be, she dismayed many of her colleagues by leaving her job to have a baby.

Unlike her academic career, Maureen did not find motherhood easy—she found it a challenge, and that it changed her perspective about what was important in life. When she eventually decided to return to work, she joined a company working to improve ways of recycling plastics. She felt that she was making a valuable contribution to society, and found the work more rewarding than the highly theoretical research she had been doing before.

Time to take stock

Jack was a trader on the stock market who had left school with one main aim: to earn a great deal of money. He enjoyed the excitement of his job, and the comfortable lifestyle it afforded him, but he worried about its instability and also felt that the pressure and stress were harming his health. He often wondered whether he should have gone to university and spent more time in choosing a career, but he found the thought of trying to make a change frightening. To avoid thinking about his problems, he habitually worked very long hours and at weekends.

When he was finally forced to take a vacation, he felt so empty that he knew he could not go back to work. Wisely, he had already saved a good nest egg, and he booked himself into a peaceful residential therapeutic center. Here, for the first time, he could really look at himself and his life, and at how he might want to change. After much thought, he decided he would set himself up as a private financial consultant, making use of his considerable contacts in the business; he knew that this way he would be able to generate enough income to live on and also have more time available so he could study music, which he had always longed to do.

Moving on

It is all too easy to feel stuck in your career; the idea of trying a new direction can seem risky and frightening, and many people feel they have too many obligations to rock the boat. Sometimes, they use their responsibilities as a smokescreen to hide their fear of change. But some kind of career shift is usually possible (see "Is Your Career on Course?" pp. 80-81). You may have to be highly creative to find innovative strategies, but if you are flexible, and have a positive outlook and a deeply rooted commitment, you can set yourself on the path toward true success—on your own terms.

Doors of opportunity
Although change is daunting, you can harness your past success to explore new directions.

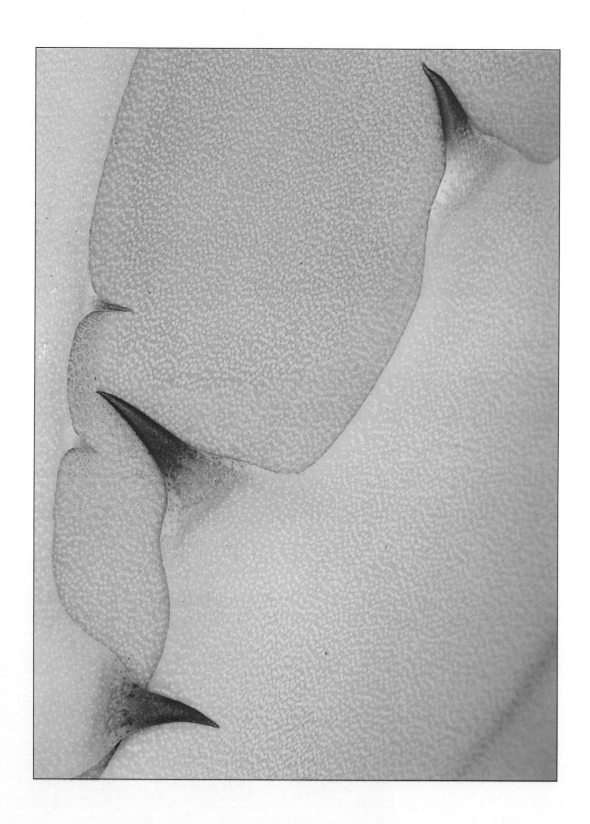

CHAPTER FOUR

OVERCOMING OBSTACLES

AS YOU CHANGE AND DEVELOP, you will have your setbacks and problems as well as triumphs and joys, but the capacity to learn from these difficulties is all part of the growing process. The questionnaire "What's Stopping You?" on pages 88-89 will help identify how you may hold yourself back from greater success and effectiveness. By becoming aware of how and why this is, you can start to behave in new, more positive ways.

Can you let yourself make mistakes? Or do you believe people will reject you if you fail? If you are to change and grow, you need to take risks; however, you may be hampered by a fear of failure (see pp. 92-93). A fear of success (pp. 94-95), which may stem from an unconscious urge to rebel against early parental pressure, or from a fear that others will envy or dislike you, can be equally limiting.

As we grow up, we are all influenced by direct and indirect messages from our families. If these messages are contradictory, you may be left with the legacy of an internal conflict that leaves you feeling confused and unable to take action. "Mixed Messages," pages 96-97, includes an exercise to help you decipher the beliefs that may be an impediment to greater joy and fulfillment.

Do you sometimes feel that you're running in circles, or that every second of the day is filled with activity? "Addicted to Action," pages 100-101, describes how we sometimes keep ourselves busy as a way to avoid really looking at our lives. Taking time out for reflection, and listening to your inner voice, will help you take stock and discover your real needs.

Although each of us has a unique perspective on the world, too great a gap between our perception and how things really are can prevent us from making the best use of our talents and resources. "Stay Tuned to Reality," pages 102-103, will help you discover if you rely too much on fantasy for fulfillment instead of focusing on tangible rewards.

When you start to make changes, others are inevitably affected, and you may find that they feel insecure and react negatively. "The Ripple Effect," pages 106-107, stresses the value of good communication for greater ease and understanding. Although others affect us, we are each responsible for our own lives. "Don't Blame—Rethink!" pages 108-109, emphasizes the importance of not blaming others—or yourself; instead, you should focus on finding your own solutions and direction for growth.

THE PROCESS OF GROWTH IS NOT WITHOUT PROBLEMS, BUT YOU

CAN USE SETBACKS TO DEEPEN YOUR SELF-KNOWLEDGE

AND TO HELP YOU TO GROW IN A MORE CONSCIOUS WAY.

WHAT'S STOPPING YOU?

Y OU FEEL FULL of optimism and energy, ready to charge ahead with your plan for a new life, a new you—yet somehow, something always seems to go wrong: The evening class you planned to do is full; you just can't make it to the gym after work; you miss the application deadline for the perfect job. Sound familiar?

You can blame the government, your boss, or your stars, but if there's a pattern of procrastination or even failure in your life, you must be responsible to some degree. You are in charge. But why would you not want to do the best for yourself? Perhaps there's a part of you that has reasons for not wanting to change (see also "Self-Defeating Behavior," pp. 110–111). This quiz will help you discover if you sabotage your efforts to grow. For each question, choose the response that most closely matches your usual behavior, note your answers, then turn to the conclusions on page 141.

1. A job is advertised internally where you work. It seems to offer everything you'd like, and you feel you have quite a good chance of getting it. Do you:
a) Find out how to apply, and do so as soon as possible so that your enthusiasm and interest come across?
b) Get further details about the job, then put off applying because you're not sure if it's what you really want after all?
c) Talk to your friends and colleagues about the good and bad points—then find you've missed the deadline?
d) Spend sleepless nights worrying about whether to apply or not, and if it would be right for you—and miss the deadline?

2. You've missed the deadline for the job you wanted. Do you feel:
a) Frustrated and angry because your career plan has been ruined and you don't know what to do?
b) Angry with yourself because you know that, if you had been wise, you could have applied for the job anyway, then decided later if it was right for you?
c) Relieved because you don't have to make a decision?
d) Dismissive, saying to yourself, "So what, it's just a job"?

3. You see a part-time evening course advertised in a subject that interests you. You can afford it, and you think you have the time. Do you:

a) Decide not to apply because it would mean that you'd have to cancel something else and alter your schedule?

b) Meet with the tutor to discuss the level of the course, but decide not to apply because you're not sure whether you liked his or her attitude that much?

c) Plan to sign up for the course if you can first persuade one of your friends to come along and take it with you?

d) Decide that you can't really afford it this year, and that you'll do it some other time?

4. At the beginning of each year, you make a list of things you resolve to change or achieve over the next 12 months. Do you:

a) Spend hours making detailed calculations, schedules, and plans?

b) Perhaps put a few plans into motion, but let them fizzle out after a while?

c) Put your list up on the bulletin board and quickly forget about it?

d) Soon lose your list?

5. When you think about the future and what it holds, do you:

a) Know in some detail what you'll be doing in the next year, almost to the day?

b) Feel you'd like to make plans but prefer to "go with the flow" because your plans may not work out?

c) Feel it's not really in your control, and that you'll worry about things as they arise?

d) No longer think about the future—you feel you'll never achieve anything anyway?

Unlock the answer
If you constantly find yourself blocked, or feel it's too difficult to initiate the changes you want in your life, discovering how you may be holding yourself back will help you alter past patterns and try new, more effective strategies.

6. When it comes to planning your annual vacation, do you find that you tend to:

a) Plan well in advance, and know exactly where you'll be going, how, and with whom? And do you organize your work load so that you complete all vital assignments before you go so that your colleagues have little to do?

b) Wait until the last minute because your work commitments never seem to run smoothly or on time, and end up going somewhere that isn't what you really wanted?

c) Intend to be more organized and plan ahead, but never do—and end up never getting away? Do you use work commitments as an excuse not to take a break?

d) Abandon your work at the last minute, preferring to take time off at home, so never go anywhere?

7. You decide you really ought to lead a healthier lifestyle and get fit. Do you:

a) Join a sports club or gym, draw up a schedule of exercise, plan a strict diet, and throw out any groceries that don't fit in with your new eating plan?

b) Start off with good intentions, get up early and go swimming a few mornings before work, then decide that it makes you feel too rushed and that you're probably not that unhealthy after all?

c) Find out about exercise classes and opening hours at your local sports club, but never get around to signing up?

d) Tell yourself that you might make the effort in summer when you'll feel more keen, but think that it's probably too late to change your ways now, and that you're just not athletic?

STUCK OR JUST RESTING?

WE ALL HAVE TIMES when we feel the need to withdraw from the world and retreat into ourselves. Sometimes this happens in a natural and spontaneous way: For example, after a tense situation has been resolved, you may feel so drained that all you want to do is sleep. At other times, the need to withdraw indicates a desire to run away, either from a problem in the external world or from feelings you'd rather not face.

It can be difficult to recognize whether retreating reflects a need for recuperation or a desire to escape, but one question to ask yourself is whether you feel refreshed or restored after your period of "rest," or whether you still have no desire or energy to face life. Harriet, for example, had been feeling "odd" for some time. She would stay in bed late whenever she could, and also took afternoon naps, but it never really made her feel any better. Then she had an argument with her best friend over something relatively trivial and burst into tears. She told her friend she didn't really know why she was crying, she just felt terribly unhappy. She hated her job and was envious of the people around her who were doing new things and going places. But the outburst in itself made Harriet realize that she had to do something about her life, and her first step was to look for a new job. Soon, the feeling of taking control gave her new enthusiasm and energy to overcome her lethargy and unhappiness.

Resting or lying low?
Many people have occasionally felt that all they want to do is take to their beds. Sometimes, this is a necessary part of the healing process, but it may also be an attempt to block out reality.

ARE YOU STUCK?

A comfortable life can easily become a trap without your realizing what has happened. If you answer "yes" to most of the following questions, you may be stuck in a rut and unsure about your next step.

• Do you feel frustrated and irritated much of the time, perhaps arguing or picking fights with friends and family?
• Do you have a constant sense of dissatisfaction—even when you succeed?
• Do you envy other people's interesting lives, but find it impossible to change your own way of life?
• Do you have a persistent feeling that you want to run away from everything and hide? Do you feel that you need to sleep a lot, or do you turn to alcohol, drugs, or food for comfort?
• Do your moods alternate between irritation and frustration, only to be followed by feelings of great futility, sadness, or hopelessness?
• Do you feel bored and restless? Do you feel that part of you wants to change, while another part is refusing to budge? Can you recognize this inner conflict?
• Do you ever act impulsively in an attempt to break free from the rut you're in?

Ring the changes
If you feel stuck or overwhelmed, reaching out for help by telephoning supportive friends or a helpline will give you the strength and insight you need to make changes.

A healthy retreat

When you feel stuck in a rut, the first thing to consider is whether this may be due to what's been going on in your life over the past year or so. Without the aid of a calendar or diary, try listing the significant events you can recall. A major life change may include personal loss—of an important relationship or your job—but it can also include positive changes, such as retiring, getting married, moving house, or having a baby. If your list includes any of these major life changes, either positive or negative, you may be experiencing the after-effects, such as anxiety or exhaustion.

After any significant experience that prompts emotional and spiritual growth or change, you may need a tranquil period in order to assimilate its meaning. If you've recently suffered an emotional trauma, you may naturally want to withdraw into yourself. This allows you to absorb and understand the experience more fully, thus integrating it into your identity. The effort of concentrating on what is occurring may leave you feeling tired, but you may also discover oases of calm security. If you're in the middle of an emotionally difficult period, you may feel exhausted, tense, and numb all at the same time. Such symptoms may be hard to bear but, with time, they do pass. If you feel tempted to take immediate, and sometimes drastic, action, bear in mind that extreme behavior or frantic activity is often a way of avoiding the difficulty of understanding yourself.

Getting unstuck

If you can recognize that you *are* stuck, then you're in a much better position to do something positive about your life than if you ignore the problem. First, you must try to understand why you are stuck. This isn't easy, because we're all adept at believing what we want to believe and find facing the truth difficult. You should also beware of changing for the sake of change, without knowing what you want to do instead. This will only lead to a vicious circle of "change-stuck-change-stuck." It may take a while before you understand the deeper feelings or motives that stop you from embracing change, but once you know how you obstruct your own growth, you'll have more power to try new ways of behaving—and can choose to be different.

FEAR OF FAILURE

What does it mean to you to fail? None of us likes to fail, but some people are far more sensitive to failure than others; what to one person may be a minor mistake may feel like a major catastrophe to someone else. Why do some people cope better than others? More importantly, how might your own reaction to failure be stopping you from doing what you want to do?

The past holds clues

At heart, a fear of failure is often a fear of how other people will react toward us if we fail, particularly those we're close to. Why do some of us expect the worst? Parents who have unreasonably high expectations of their children often have a low sense of self-esteem, and need to see their children as extensions of themselves who will provide the self-confidence they lack. Such parents may insist that their children always do well in school, always look neat and clean, and never make mistakes; in other words, they must never fail at anything. If the parent responds to the child when he or she "fails" by withdrawing affection, unreasonable punishment, or by more threatening behavior, that child will equate failure with loss of love, and carry that fear into adulthood.

Are you good enough?
We model our future behavior by being inspired or challenged by people we admire or respect. Sometimes, however, we inhibit our progress because we don't acknowledge our own talents.

How others see us

Some people measure themselves by the expectations of others. We all do this to some extent out of a need to be loved and accepted. If this is carried to an extreme, however, we risk losing our sense of identity, and with it our self-worth. Very insecure people may try, often unconsciously, to work out how to behave so that they never disappoint what they assume are other people's expectations; they then become excessively timid, meek, and subservient. Very often, the assumptions about other people's feelings are based on fear and may thus be distorted; the result may be that the person who is afraid of failing may be living in a prison of his or her own making, with little contact with the real world.

How we cope with failure

How you feel about the mistakes you make, or have made, influences how you expect others to feel. If, for example, you think failure is unforgivable, you will assume that everyone around you feels the same way. However, other people may be far more tolerant of your failures and mistakes than you are of yourself. By being unforgiving of yourself, you make other people into your "enemies" who will judge you harshly; in reality, you may be your own worst enemy.

A sense of self-worth is created by taking risks—not all of which will be successful. Someone who is very sensitive to failure will retreat from taking risks in order to avoid feeling ashamed, humiliated, or unlovable. Thus a vicious circle is created: Risk-taking is avoided in order to avoid failure, and self-esteem never grows.

A deeper feeling of failure may come from not living up to your own personal standards and moral code. You may sense that somehow you're not conducting your life in the way you know you could. The awareness that you're capable of more, that you're not living your life as the person you really are, can prompt you to want to grow and to change.

Ironically, the fear of failure can sometimes be due to an inflated sense of self-importance. The person who doesn't allow him- or herself to fail may also be someone who needs to be seen as perfect. Maintaining this image is very hard work, and may sabotage any attempt at self-development, which inevitably involves making mistakes.

Learning to fail

To overcome a fear of failure, try not to see it as the opposite of success—such a black-and-white view doesn't allow for the subtleties of real life. Too often, we overlook or dismiss the fact that it takes great courage to try and to risk failure. To try something, even if you fail in your ultimate aim, is in itself a success. Start by choosing something you want to do that doesn't have serious consequences. Perhaps you want to learn how to swim, but make up excuses to hide your fear that you won't be any good at it. Do it now! You will undoubtedly learn something and be more confident for trying. It doesn't matter that you may never become a great swimmer, but you'll probably know how to save yourself from drowning. Most importantly, you'll discover that most fears are unfounded and, with time and awareness, can be overcome.

Overcoming hurdles
No matter how confident you are, facing new challenges can be daunting, but it's better to do your best than to do nothing.

93

FEAR OF SUCCESS

You may believe that you're working your hardest to get ahead and to achieve your goals, but if you never quite succeed, you may need to ask yourself what might be holding you back—it could be the prospect of success itself. Many of us have been pressured in one way or another to reach for the top. The pressure to succeed may overtake the enthusiasm to fulfill the goal, so that the goal to be the best becomes the only thing that matters. Also, deep down, we may feel that we are worthy or lovable only if we achieve, rather than if we are just ourselves. There may be no enjoyment of achievements, and no real contentment when so-called success is achieved.

Self-sabotage

Sometimes, a refusal to succeed can be a way of rebelling against the wishes of your parents or other authority figures—even if they no longer directly influence your life. You may be trying to get back at them, perhaps due to unresolved anger or resentment because you were rejected or felt unloved. You may consciously try your hardest to succeed at something, but on an unconscious level you may be saying, "I'm willing to sacrifice what I want most in order *not* to please them." Such self-sabotage "succeeds" through failure. An example of this is the teenager who is perfectly able to do well at school, but sets about failing in order to spite his or her parents. This process is usually not at all conscious. In the end, both child and parents suffer; but for the teenager—and often for many adults—failing his or her parents' expectations takes priority over their own wish to succeed.

Although we're encouraged to believe that success, particularly material success, is a good thing, there is often an underlying, and contradictory, message that success is wrong because it leads to arrogance and selfishness. We may also be taught that to admit openly to want to be the best is wrong, and that we will incur the dislike of those around us. As children, we are often faced by a difficult decision: to fail and be punished by our parents, or succeed but risk being disliked by our peer group for succeeding. The end result is that we "choose" to fail in order to avoid success because it appears to be the lesser of two evils. As adults, we may be unaware that we're still acting this way.

Fear of competition
In an attempt to free themselves from parental pressure, some people may unconsciously refuse to excel.

ON SAFE GROUND?

If you never seem to reach your goals despite your constant pursuit of them, and you feel frustrated because you know you've got what it takes, you may be stuck on what looks like safe ground. For people whose self-esteem is dependent on outside sources of success and failure, this is a common problem. The hidden fear may be that to strive for success—and achieve it—is to risk subsequent failure, so it's better not to succeed at all. Only by facing your fear will you get beyond it. The only failure is the failure to try.

There are some people who enjoy the experience of being envied for their success because it gives them a sense of power. This, however, is a very precarious source of self-worth because when others no longer envy them, there is a critical loss of self-esteem. Success may also feed an obsession to stay on top at all costs, which can contribute to ruthless and self-serving behavior; failure may then lead to overwhelming feelings of hopelessness and self-loathing. Many a famous person has broken down under the strain of success—or, more usually, the waning of success.

Know your worth

Another common reason for failing to achieve your potential may be because, on either a conscious or unconscious level, you don't believe you *deserve* to succeed. The tell-tale signs that you may feel like this include not being able to be kind to yourself, difficulty in accepting compliments or gifts, or feeling a need to punish and criticize yourself. You may feel driven to succeed in order to justify your existence—which has little to do with real self-fulfillment—or so fear failure that you never risk anything new because it may lead to feelings of shame or humiliation.

The fear of not being able to stay on top, or of arousing people's envy and dislike, or of not deserving success, may be inhibiting you from taking risks. Try asking yourself what it is that you fear, and try to discover the origin of your fear. Then, instead of repeating all these negative reasons, concentrate on the strengths you *do* have and the reasons why you deserve to succeed. Your goals will then be much easier to achieve.

Lonely at the top

There's no doubt that it takes a strong personality and plenty of self-confidence to compete for a top job in a competitive field. Being a success may also mean being able to tolerate the not-very-generous feelings of others, especially their envy. If you tend to be envious of other people's success, you'll probably fear that they will feel the same toward you.

MIXED MESSAGES

DID YOUR PARENTS EVER SAY, "Open wide!" before giving you medicine? Did you have any choice in the matter, or did you simply swallow it? Until you got a bit older, you probably "swallowed" most parental messages whole; you weren't in a position to say, "Wait a minute, I need to think about that…"

Most messages we received in childhood come from the people we depended on for our survival, and for this reason they are extremely powerful and deeply rooted, even if we aren't aware of them.

Conflict and confusion

In general, these messages don't cause a problem; they help us to take care of ourselves and of other people. Only if we have received contradictory, confusing messages, or when our adult needs and desires conflict with the messages we learned in childhood, do we find ourselves in trouble.

For example, Sally's mother came from a poor family, and always told Sally to save as much as possible, and never indulge herself. Sally's father came from a financially secure family, and his mother spent money freely on her children. He in turn spoiled his own children. His message was, "Enjoy life while you can," while his wife's was, "Spend today and you'll regret it tomorrow." As a result, although Sally was well paid, she was unsure how to handle money; if she spent it, even on "serious" purchases such as a car, she felt guilty and got no pleasure from it.

Sometimes the inherited message so overburdens a child that, instead of guiding him or her, it generates the opposite behavior. Harold's parents encouraged the belief that success was the only thing worth having; for them, success was measured simply by status rather than personal fulfillment. Harold was encouraged to be a doctor or lawyer, but even though he was very intelligent and a hard worker once he committed himself to a task, he couldn't focus on one direction and spent many years drifting aimlessly from job to job until he recognized that he was unconsciously rebelling against parental pressure.

Who do you see?

Your sense of self is influenced by the responses you receive from other people; most are meant to be supportive—others can be confusing.

96

Past messages, present muddles

The messages you received as a child can profoundly affect your adult life. You may be confused, like Sally, or, like Harold, may find it difficult to move forward and find fulfillment because one part of you (the parental voice) is saying, "Do as you're told!" while the other part (your own voice) is saying, "No, I won't!" The result is stalemate, which for some people may lead to years of feeling stuck and unhappy. Messages from your parents are particularly powerful, but they may not be how *you* really feel or want to feel.

The important thing to recognize is that contradictory messages don't just cancel each other out; they are absorbed, whether consciously or not, and become part of you, creating what may be intense internal conflict, particularly when you need to make important life decisions such as choosing a career or a marital partner. Faced with such a dilemma, the "solution" to such conflict for many people is to do nothing at all, which only increases their feelings of helplessness and frustration.

Unmixing the messages

If you feel stuck or indecisive, you're probably struggling with conflicting messages. To resolve your dilemma, try writing down the different voices that carry the messages: Identify who is "speaking," the tone of voice, and the circumstances in which the voice speaks. Then rephrase the message so that it more accurately reflects *your* thoughts or aspirations. If, for example, one voice says, "You're only a worthwhile person if you're very wealthy," try rephrasing it so that the voice says , "I'm a worthwhile person because I'm conscientious and good at what I do."

With practice, you'll find it easier to unravel the potent messages from childhood, and so become more aware of why you feel confused, stuck, or indecisive. The more you understand of the past, the freer you are to move on. Your range of present choices will enlarge so that you can be the person you want to be.

CHANGING SLOWLY

GREAT TECHNOLOGICAL ADVANCES in the past few decades have dramatically altered our everyday lives, enabling us to do many things in half the time it took our parents to do them: We can cross a continent in a single day, access information in another country at the touch of a button, or make instant contact with someone far away. In a world where we can expect instant results in our professional lives, it is tempting to expect the same in our personal lives once we have decided to change.

Patience to grow

It's taken your whole life so far for you to become the complex person you are today, so why should you expect to change deeply entrenched behavior and attitudes overnight? Try thinking of yourself as having a child within you, perhaps a confused or apprehensive one, who may need gentle coaxing and understanding. To rush this child into new situations that may be terrifying or confusing will only cause him or her to withdraw. For every part of you that wants to grow, there is probably another, sometimes bigger, part saying, "No! I don't want to!" Just as a child will respond to impatience and anger by becoming stubborn or upset, so will your more vulnerable self—so learn to treat yourself with patience and gentleness.

In at the deep end?

Trying to make real changes in your life can be scary and frustrating; in an attempt to avoid such painful reality, it's a common mistake to jump into the deep end before testing the water—or even knowing if you can swim. You may be tempted to rush in head-first to "get it over with"—so you leave your partner, quit your job, sell your house, and turn your life upside down.

Do it in stages
Any great change, such as redecorating your home, probably can't be accomplished in one day. Making progress in gradual stages allows you to pace yourself, and to reconsider your plan if things don't go smoothly.

Often it's when you feel most trapped or you're in a situation you can't bear that you want to move very quickly. It doesn't work. A change that is most likely to last comes from taking small steps, slowly gaining confidence and understanding as you go. Give yourself the chance to assimilate the changes slowly and thoroughly. This can take much longer than you expected, but you should not be impatient with yourself, or lose hope.

Listen to your inner voice

Don't put pressure on yourself to change faster than you can. As soon as you're aware of a part of you that's fighting against change, stop and listen carefully and uncritically. Ask yourself questions such as, "Why don't I want to do this? What is it that's frightening me?" "Why am I holding myself back?" By listening to the part of yourself that doesn't want to change, you can keep your steady growth on course.

It's common to feel anxious about where you're going and whether it's the right direction, and you may lose sight of the fact that you're in the process of growing—but you are.

Be patient

We often plunge into action before setting time aside to think about things and to listen to our inner voice. If it says, for example, "I'm lonely," or "I don't know who I am or what I want," you might feel frightened, or suddenly decide to act too soon as a way of escaping from anxiety. Changing slowly means being able to tolerate periods of solitude and uncertainty, and sometimes feeling panicky or even sad. By developing the strength to tolerate these uncomfortable feelings, you will not rush into things too quickly, and can make real progress.

STEPS TO CHANGE

By nature, personal growth is an unpredictable process, and no two people change and develop in exactly the same way or at the same pace. At times you will want to take giant strides, and make dynamic changes; at other times, you will want to proceed in tiny steps or proceed with caution. There is no right or wrong way—you just need to discover what's right for you and to be flexible to the demands of the situation.

Leaping ahead

• Take care to pace yourself. If you tend to live life at a hectic pace, you may accomplish a great deal, but still be unclear about your real long-term needs and goals. Your vitality is a great asset so long as you don't use activity as a way of blocking the demands of your inner voice.
• When you're feeling positive and full of energy, you may want to surge ahead; this is fine, but take care that you don't exhaust your energies and run out of steam.

Taking your time

• To get in touch with your real self requires patience and stillness, so you will need to tune in to your inner voice to discover when to move ahead, slow down, or stop and take stock.
• If you're frightened, think about what it is that frightens you. When you're ready, start again. Slowly, you'll become aware of the subtle changes taking place in you, which will give you the inspiration and confidence you need to take the next step.

ADDICTED TO ACTION

If you're active all the time, it's easy to convince yourself and others that you're doing important and constructive things; it can also be an effective way of avoiding really looking at yourself, your life, and where you're heading. Often, we avoid the deeper issues we need to deal with because we fear they may create too much pain and confusion, and one of the ways we do this is by keeping busy. A well-known reaction to sudden loss and trauma, for example, is to move into overdrive. You may have experienced this yourself: cleaning the house from top to bottom, going to the gym more than usual, socializing continuously. Sometimes people say that all this activity is a way of burning off excess energy; more likely, it's a way of avoiding confronting the pain of loss.

Face your feelings

In terms of personal growth, effective action and healthy change may come only after a long period of reflection and self-questioning. Although sometimes it is necessary to move ahead quickly and to face the consequences later on, if your life is consistently overfilled with activity, it's likely that you're avoiding real change. You need to stop running in circles in order to find out what the real issues are and what you need to do.

In many cases, it's only when we're forced to stop that we come face to face with the feelings we're trying to avoid. People who are frantic "doers" often run themselves ragged; they may then fall ill or have an accident, which forces them to take stock and evaluate their life situation. It's as if their bodies and minds are telling them they need to stop and pay attention to what is happening to them.

Going nowhere fast?
You may find yourself frantically doing the same things over and over as a way of avoiding feelings.

Learning to be alone

One way to avoid overactivity is to assess how much time you allow yourself to be alone. If you tend to fill every minute of the day, you may deliberately have to set aside time alone for "doing nothing." Start with half an hour two or three times a week. Unplug the telephone, turn off the television and radio. Try relaxation exercises, or simply sit or lie down and let your thoughts wander. If you find it impossible, reduce the amount of time to start with, but work toward increasing it. The important thing is that you gradually get used to feeling comfortable with your thoughts and without distractions.

Assess your activities

Look at the activities in your life, and at what you do with your time. Ask yourself: Do I really enjoy doing these activities, or are they simply "fillers"? Do I look forward to meeting people I've planned to see? Do I have to work late every night? We often have catastrophic, and unrealistic, expectations of what will happen if we change our behavior, fearing that a change in our habits may alienate our friends or our family. People who use activity to avoid being alone may act as if the world would stop spinning if they didn't keep on the go. They need to acknowledge that they have their own personal reasons for behaving in this way rather than attributing it to external circumstances.

Although you may find it hard in the beginning to change your habitual way of behaving—and many of us are afraid to change—you will probably come to enjoy, and need, your time alone. Allow yourself the space and time to reflect, and you may be surprised by the thoughts and ideas that come to you. As well as having the power to be immensely restorative of both physical and mental energies, a long stretch of deep, uninterrupted silence provides a way of listening to yourself, so that you can discover who you are and what you really need.

STOP AND THINK

How do you know if you're addicted to action? If you agree with over half of the following statements, you may need to consider if such frantic activity is a means of running away from particular problems or feelings.

- I'm generally on the go from the time I get up until I go to bed, with few breaks to catch my breath or relax.
- I plan my days and evenings so that I'm rarely on my own—because if I'm alone, I tend to feel anxious, ill at ease, and sometimes frightened.
- My weekends are as busy as my weekdays.
- I find it difficult, if not impossible, to sit still and do nothing. I often do two things at once.
- When I'm faced with an unexpected period of time alone, I immediately fill it with an activity.
- During times alone, I feel a need to do something: clean the house, watch television, or call a friend.

Some people feel guilty if they aren't always on the go, as if they need to justify their existence by "doing"; without constant activity, they feel empty, and have little or no sense of self-worth. Those who use activity as a solution often had parents who encouraged them not to look too deeply into themselves; "don't think," was the message they were taught, "keep busy." For some people, inactivity and reflection can trigger anxiety and depression. The more extreme the reaction, the deeper the fear of confronting the real problem or suppressed feelings. If you become deeply anxious or overwhelmed by feelings of sadness when you're alone, you may want to consider outside help such as counseling or therapy. Otherwise, it may be a matter of working slowly to change your habitual behavior. You could begin by setting aside time for quiet reflection each day, perhaps going for a walk or keeping a journal of your most personal thoughts.

STAY TUNED TO REALITY

If you feel warm but a friend says she feels cold, who's right? Most of us would accept that, to some degree, reality is in the eye of the beholder. However, if there is too great a distortion between your perception of reality and things as they really *are*, life will be frustrating. People who have a clear grasp of reality find it easier to grow and change, and to reach their true potential, so it's important to achieve a balanced view of life—using your fantasies to inspire you, but being able to recognize opportunities for growth in the real world.

Your view of reality

When you watch a movie, you build up a picture of "reality" based on all the information and clues you are given. Then you discover that you have only been given selective information, or misread the signs, and the picture you have created is distorted—the hero is, in fact, the villain and about to lead the heroine into a fatal trap. In real life, we cling even more firmly to our picture of reality, and can be surprisingly unreceptive to information that might change this view. If a couple whom we always believed to be blissfully happy announce their divorce, we may feel that they were deceiving us; perhaps they hid their unhappiness from us, or the signs may have been there but we didn't recognize them or chose to ignore them.

Your interpretation of reality—your view of the world—is affected by many factors, such as your culture, past, prejudices, beliefs, expectations, emotions, physical makeup, and the information you are given. Reality is also colored by your view of yourself. When you're feeling low, everything around you looks unappealing, even intimidating; on other days, when you feel good, everything else looks good, too. The reality is usually a mixture: both satisfaction and disappointment, success and failure.

Self-confidence and self-worth

If you have a sense of self-worth, you will be able to view the world reasonably clearly and without undue distortion. You will not be consumed by grandiose fantasies and overestimate your abilities, nor will you be too daunted in the face of challenges. If you reach too high and are knocked down, you can accept this as a setback, not as a judgment about whether you are a "good" or a "bad" person.

People with low self-esteem often find failure more difficult to bear, and in order to avoid this pain, they may resort to a distorted fantasy life. Jane, for example, harbored a secret fantasy that she was superior to her friends and colleagues. Because she believed she was destined for wealth and success, Jane felt she didn't have to exert herself; all she had to do was wait to be "discovered." As a result, she never thought about improving her work skills.

Larry, on the other hand, was convinced that he was a failure. When his employers praised his work, he believed it was because they pitied him, not that he had done anything worthwhile. He was also convinced he would fail at anything he tried, and so took few risks. Both an inferiority or a superiority complex may be a sign of a distorted fantasy life.

Use your fantasies

You can use your fantasy life as a source of clues about who you are and what you want from life. Your daydreams can reveal kernels of valuable truth. For example, if you dream of being a mountaineer, try to analyze exactly what it is about the fantasy that appeals to you. Is it the idea of escaping from your present life? Or the thought of really testing yourself? Is it the physical challenge? Feeling in harmony with the natural world? Is your fantasy achievable? Are there elements—challenge, being outdoors, taking risks—that you could introduce into your present life and work? Analyzing your fantasy will help you come up with a realistic plan for meeting your inner needs and desires—and the clue that helps you achieve your ultimate goal.

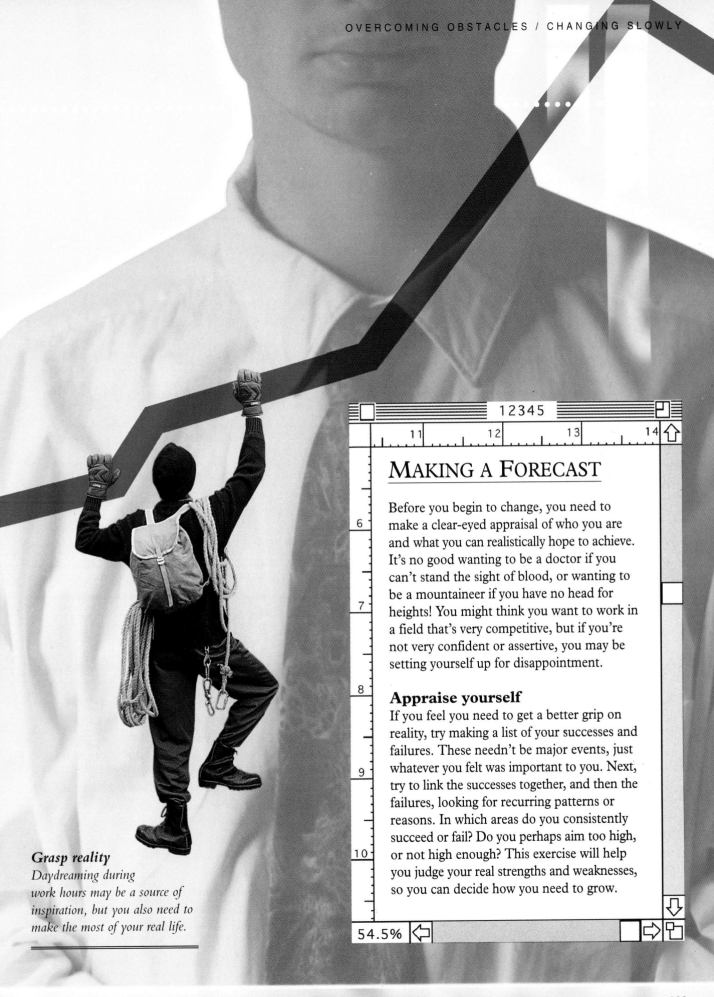

Grasp reality
*Daydreaming during
work hours may be a source of
inspiration, but you also need to
make the most of your real life.*

12345

11   12   13   14

MAKING A FORECAST

Before you begin to change, you need to
make a clear-eyed appraisal of who you are
and what you can realistically hope to achieve.
It's no good wanting to be a doctor if you
can't stand the sight of blood, or wanting to
be a mountaineer if you have no head for
heights! You might think you want to work in
a field that's very competitive, but if you're
not very confident or assertive, you may be
setting yourself up for disappointment.

Appraise yourself
If you feel you need to get a better grip on
reality, try making a list of your successes and
failures. These needn't be major events, just
whatever you felt was important to you. Next,
try to link the successes together, and then the
failures, looking for recurring patterns or
reasons. In which areas do you consistently
succeed or fail? Do you perhaps aim too high,
or not high enough? This exercise will help
you judge your real strengths and weaknesses,
so you can decide how you need to grow.

54.5%

WANTING OR NEEDING?

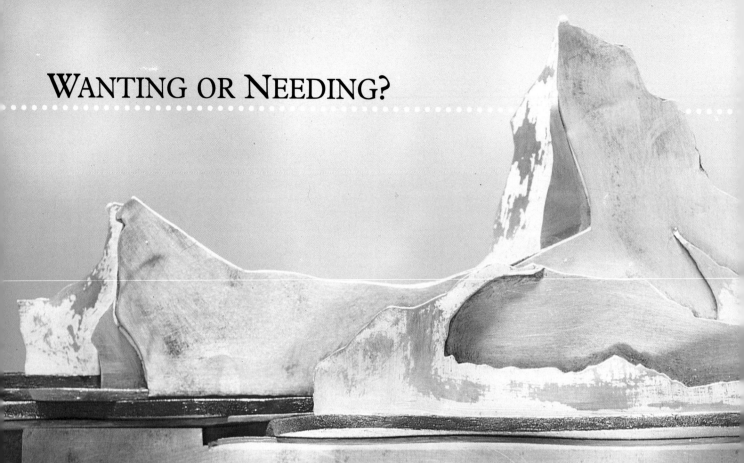

Although many of us often use the words "want" and "need" interchangeably, they actually mean very different things. *Wants* are conscious desires, appetites, or wishes—we want a larger house, or to earn more money, or to achieve greater professional recognition. *Needs* are usually more urgent and essential—we *need* food and shelter in order to survive; we need love and affection to thrive. Needs may also arise from strong urges or emotional or psychological deficiencies that must be satisfied. You may be unconscious of some of your needs, and it's quite possible to spend years in pursuit of what you think you want without getting close to what you really need to feel fulfilled. When you reach a point where you feel stuck, it's time to question what your real needs are.

Buried needs

If what you needed as a child was consistently refused you, or if you were repeatedly punished or reprimanded, you may well have grown up believing that some of your needs were bad or wrong. For instance, every time Robert went to his mother for a hug, she would push him away and say, "Not now! Can't you see I'm busy?" Starved of affection, Robert became an aloof, lonely man. Sally was another lonely person who, as a child, was afraid of the dark. She needed reassurance, but instead was told to stop being a "baby" and to grow up. Later,

she became an independent, self-sufficient young woman who was outwardly confident and had many acquaintances, but was actually ashamed of being afraid of people; she was also terrified of intimacy. Both Robert and Sally had buried needs that they were struggling to hide: Robert needed love and affection, while Sally needed to feel safe. Only by acknowledging their long-repressed needs would they begin to feel less lonely.

What do you really need?

Sometimes, what we're taught we *should* want is not what we really need. For example, you may have been taught that money and prestige are the most important things in life, but your sense of fulfillment may depend on an inner need to help others. Or you could be so set in your belief that you need to be successful that it undermines your personal relationships; you might then discover that success means little to you because you're lonely.

If your needs go unmet, unacknowledged disappointment, sadness, or frustration may impede your personal growth. For instance, if you need to feel in control of your life to satisfy a deeper need to feel safe, you might be fearful of trying new things—so you may reach an impasse and end up feeling stuck. If you need to be "right" all the time, you may be afraid of failure, and so never try any of the things that would really make you happy.

Look below the surface
Your real needs may be obscured by the image you have of yourself, possibly in response to other people's expectations. To get in touch with your real needs, you need to look deeper inside yourself.

You need courage

The more you know yourself, the easier it is to work on your personal growth. Self-knowledge, however, requires honesty, which can feel uncomfortable. You may not like to admit that you're lonely or feel empty, especially if you strive to appear very sure of yourself, and it might be difficult to acknowledge that you don't really know yourself or your needs. It takes courage to admit this to yourself and to others, but it's often an essential first step if you want to change.

Sometimes, needs that are unrealistic—a need to be perfect, to be in control at all times, to be loved completely and by everyone, for example—can be rechanneled. By becoming more aware, it is possible to harness the energy behind these needs and divert them to more constructive, useful areas: for example, the driven energy of perfectionism might be hard for your family to live with, but a great asset if you are a graphic designer or a surgeon.

How you choose to deal with your needs is entirely in your hands. The more you can discover and accept your real needs, the better chance you have of gratifying them. First, however, you must look deep into yourself and find out what these needs are, why you have them, and whether you *want* to fulfill them. With understanding comes greater freedom to choose how to act—and this freedom in turn provides the chance for growth.

FEEL YOUR NEEDS

You can get more in touch with your real needs by taking time to think about your feelings. Start by identifying obvious needs that you can respond to easily. You may find it easier if you think about needs for different aspects of yourself, and ask yourself prompting questions. Are your needs:

• **Physical:** Are you tired? Do you need an early night? A long, relaxing bath with scented oil? How does your body feel—do you need some exercise to invigorate you, or a healthier diet?

• **Emotional/psychological:** Are your relationships rewarding? Would you like greater intimacy or more open communication?

• **Social:** Do you feel isolated? Do you need to work on improving your friendships, or on being more involved with your community?

• **Creative:** Would you like more of an outlet for your creativity? If you need to express yourself creatively, how could you do this?

• **Intellectual:** Are you sufficiently stimulated mentally? Could you expand your reading, or develop friendships with more people of different lifestyles, views, and opinions?

• **Spiritual:** Are your inner/spiritual needs met? Can you take time on your own to explore them?

THE RIPPLE EFFECT

We are all affected by the people around us, and we, in turn, affect others. As the English poet John Donne wrote: "No man is an island, entire of itself…" Because none of us exists in isolation, your actions have an impact on the people you know and love; it is important to both accept and expect this, because if you start making changes in your life, it may have a knock-on effect on them—and this may make them anxious, fearful, or insecure.

What do you expect?

The process of change often starts in your imagination. You think about making a change and picture how others might react or feel about what you decide to do. How you envisage others' reactions can either help or hinder you in taking the plunge, even if it's only a relatively minor change. For example, if you want to be more assertive, but have a mental picture of your partner reacting angrily, you'll be less likely to try out this new approach than if you imagine him or her showing approval of the new, more confident you.

If you're very sensitive about other people's opinions and feelings, you may find it especially difficult to change your behavior, fearing that their feelings toward you might change. However, if you sacrifice your own happiness and needs in order to be approved of and loved, you'll end up feeling frustrated, resentful, or angry. You may get stuck: unable to go forward and make the changes you want, yet dissatisfied with the old patterns.

Resisting change

Many people cling to old habits because predictability makes us feel safe and in control. Even if certain patterns limit our potential for happiness and personal development, the need to feel secure and to stick with what is familiar may be paramount. For example, a mother who always puts the needs of her family before her own might fear losing their approval if she started to take greater care of her own needs; her partner and family might also resist such a change, fearing her behavior means she loves them less. Many partnerships falter at this point. Both people may be miserable, but neither is willing to change because it means risking the security of the "couple." When safety takes priority over growth and change, a relationship may reach a stalemate.

Spot the sabotage

Other people may resist your attempts to change by trying to undermine you in such a subtle way that neither of you is fully aware of it. There might be support and encouragement on the surface, but signs of mixed feelings might appear in the form of unexpected or unfair criticism; or you might find that someone withholds important messages.

For example, when Ann got a job that involved traveling, her partner became critical of certain aspects of her behavior: the clothes she wore, the meals she cooked, even the way she closed a door. Because he felt unable to voice his concern over her long hours, and his fear of abandonment and envy of her success—and he may not have been aware of these feelings—he expressed them in other ways.

Emotional crosscurrents
We are all separate individuals, yet our actions and responses have an effect on those around us as well as on ourselves.

Envy

If you have friends who are stuck and are unhappy or frustrated with their own lives, they may become envious of you for doing what they feel unable to do. Misery loves company, and your friends might be afraid they'll lose the comfort of being with someone who is as stuck as they are, someone with whom they can spend time voicing their resentment, or complaining about how "unfair" life is instead of trying to create their own opportunities. Your decision to change and get on with your life may make them question aspects of their own lives and behavior, but also make them painfully aware that they are unable or afraid to change. If you wish to sustain the relationship, it may be necessary to reassure them that you still care for and value them.

The fear of loss

In intimate relationships, a fear of change—on both sides—is often a fear of losing the other person. Your partner might imagine that if you break the familiar pattern, there's a risk you won't want him or her anymore; surprisingly, the person making the change often has a similar fear. Anything that threatens our need to feel loved and wanted, even if in the long term it's in the best interests of both parties, will feel dangerous.

How secure your intimates are will determine how safe they feel about your changing. If they don't feel they can trust your love for them, they'll be afraid of losing you. If they feel confident that they won't lose you, and that you still value them, they'll be more willing to support and encourage you.

CHANGING WITH CARE

Knowing and understanding that people fear change because they fear loss should help you to change with care. Acknowledge and accept the feelings of others without giving up your desire to change and grow. If you don't understand someone's fears or anxieties, there's a danger that you'll give in out of guilt or fear, and abandon your plans for change. Remember, the deeper someone's fear of losing you, the more intense will be their anger, hurt, or criticism.

Talk to those around you, explaining—many times, if necessary—how and why you've decided to change. Others need to be reminded that you're changing in order to help yourself, not to hurt them.

Stay firm in your intention to continue; you might need to say that although you would prefer that they support you, it won't stop you if they don't. If they try to block you with threats, you will have to decide what is more important, and choose between making your intended change or sacrificing what you want in order to maintain the status quo. Sometimes the best course of action is to let things calm down for a while, and then continue on your course of change. Remember these helpful points:
• Don't criticize those around you for not changing, just because you have decided to.
• Try not to be defensive or aggressive. You don't have to justify your decision to change.
• Keep an open mind; don't *expect* others to react negatively to the changes you make.
• If you sense others' fears or anger, try to bring the problem out in the open. Ask them directly how they feel about the way you're changing.

DON'T BLAME—RETHINK!

BLAMING OTHER PEOPLE or outside factors for our problems is something we all do at times: We blame our low mood on the weather, or on the fact that we have a cold, or on our boss for reprimanding us for being late. Usually, we can admit that apportioning blame like this is a strategy for temporarily letting ourselves off the hook. Some people, however, blame others for their own unhappiness as a way to avoid taking responsibility for themselves. They may have no real desire to improve their situation or change. If you know someone like this, you probably find it very tiring to be in their company for long; it's easy to lose sympathy for a person when you sense that their fault-finding is an end in itself.

For example, Martha had decided that the source of all her problems was her mother. When friends suggested she do something positive herself to tackle her problems—her inability to keep a job, to find a partner, to control her weight—Martha accused them of not understanding: It wasn't her fault, it was her mother's, and there was nothing she could do.

Tempting targets?
It's often easier to target other people or circumstances as the source of your troubles, but blaming won't help you change or bring you greater fulfillment.

Grievances are dangerous

If you hold others responsible for your problems, it can become a habit that's hard to break. It can become part of your identity and way of life, giving you a spurious sense of security. To give up the "blaming" attitude would mean abandoning the main way you deal with the world.

The need to hang on to anger and get even runs deep in many people, and can strongly influence our thoughts and feelings. Often, we may not be aware of our desire to make someone else suffer for our own unhappiness. When happiness takes second place to a desire for revenge, it is known as "secondary gain." Vital energy, which could be directed toward growth, is drained by the need to see someone else suffer.

Colin, for example, grew up in a family where pressure was put on all the children to be successful. As a child, Colin developed mysterious allergies; as an adolescent, he was very troubled and unable to attend school much of the time. At university, he developed chronic fatigue syndrome, and dropped out, returning to live with his parents. We often use our bodies to communicate feelings we can't express directly; Colin's ill health may well have originated in his feeling that he never received the care and attention he needed as a child. Avoiding success through illness was also a way of getting back at his parents. By becoming ill, he was ensuring he got the attention he wanted, but to do this he was sacrificing his own desire to learn and grow.

A negative alliance

In close relationships, there is a risk of collusion; that is, both parties unconsciously agree to foster an unhealthy attitude or way of behaving. For example, a person who drinks to blot out his or her unhappiness might make other family members feel that family responsibilities and pressure are the "cause" of the excessive drinking. The family, for their part, may collude by making that person a scapegoat for all family problems, rather than looking at how the family operates as a whole. This type of destructive behavior only stops when one side refuses to play the game, takes responsibility for his or her part in it, and insists that the other person also take responsibility for what is mutually destructive behavior. Change can then occur.

Be an adult

Taking responsibility for yourself means accepting that you have the means to influence and direct your behavior in appropriate and positive ways. It also means having the courage to look at your situation and acknowledge that you may be contributing to your own unhappiness.

Acting like an adult, instead of a wounded child, means clearing the decks of all blame—including self-blame—and deciding you have the strength to change. Accept that the past can be a source of understanding who you are, and not the reason for assigning blame or refusing to change. You might know that you weren't treated well as a child, or that something happened to you that contributed

to your being the way you are. This is valuable information that you can use to help you grow, but it won't help you if you remain angry and resentful. Be honest with yourself and stay on the alert for the part of you that wants to slide back into passing the buck. You have the power to free yourself— you can't change the past, but you can make a choice to learn from it and to move on, focusing on the present and future that you really want and have the potential to create.

IT'S ALL MY FAULT!

Blaming others can be a way of avoiding the pain of guilt and regret. To acknowledge that you have hurt others, or to accept that you're not living up to your real potential, can be a source of anguish.

In the process of reclaiming responsibility for yourself, there's a danger that you will swing from blaming others to blaming yourself. Although we often swing between these two attitudes, both are ways of avoiding responsibility and of inhibiting understanding and true growth. The point of self-awareness is not to find out who did what to whom, or who is at fault, but simply to understand why your life is unfulfilling. If you focus solely on blame, you can't focus on growth, on what you really want to do, and on how to get to where you want to be.

Do you blame yourself?
Self-blame may make you feel virtuous or martyred, but it won't make you happy. Take responsibility for your actions, but focus on the changes you want to make, not on past mistakes.

SELF-DEFEATING BEHAVIOR

D o you find that, however much you long to be successful, your plans never come to anything, and you don't ever seem to get what you really want or need? It may be that, without knowing it, you are actually preventing yourself from being successful. The causes of self-defeating behavior can be difficult to unravel, and although you may be able to spot such behavior in others, it can be hard to recognize in yourself. You may be aware of feelings of self-doubt, self-hatred, and guilt, or perhaps you feel depressed and defeated. Or you may only be aware that you're unhappy—not that you're contributing to your own unhappiness.

Destructive guilt

Even people who are successful and achieve their goals may unconsciously sabotage their achievements later on because of a sense of guilt. There are many reasons for feeling guilt, such as an inability to accept and learn from previous mistakes and put them behind you, which may cause you unconsciously to repeat them; this type of behavior is known as repetition compulsion. Guilt is also caused by self-doubt or self-hatred. For example, you may be on the point of completing something good when, strangely, it all goes wrong; or you make plans to do something positive for yourself but then feel pressured to give them up. Ask yourself whether you might be making this happen, and if so, why? You will find it impossible to give to yourself if you feel deep inside that you don't deserve anything, or that you're somehow bad and need to be punished.

Healthy and unhealthy parts

While most of the time you focus your energies on doing things to help yourself, there may be a small but powerful part of your inner self that actively works against you. It may be an inner voice that says things like, "Why bother? I'm bound to fail," or "I really shouldn't be doing this, I don't deserve it." This voice is that part of your personality that Freud

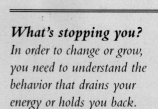

What's stopping you?
In order to change or grow, you need to understand the behavior that drains your energy or holds you back.

DO YOU DEFEAT YOURSELF?

Being aware of self-defeating behavior is the first step toward taking control of your life. If you answer "yes" to any of the following questions, you may be locked in patterns of behavior that are undermining your efforts to grow and change:

• Do you deliberately take on too much, thus ensuring that you'll fail?
• Do you make promises to yourself and others that you know you can't fulfill?
• Do you push yourself too hard, thus ensuring that you don't have the physical and emotional stamina to carry out all the tasks you've set yourself?

• Do you take on too little because you have no great faith in your abilities?
• Are you easily swayed by other people?
• Do you always find last-minute excuses for not doing things—for example, suddenly deciding that other people's needs are more pressing than yours?
• Are you trying to hurt someone else with your lack of success? Is it worth the effort?
• Do you feel you don't deserve to help yourself? Underlying guilt may be stopping you from changing.
• Is it possible that you're afraid of success or failure (see also pp. 92-95)? Self-defeating behavior can result from a fear of one or the other, or of both.

called the superego, the voice coming from someone you regard as an authority figure (perhaps a parent or teacher). Some people who have a very demanding superego have extremely rigorous standards of behavior, which they often feel they can never meet. They may then drive themselves too hard, becoming relentless perfectionists who find it impossible to do anything without feeling inadequate—and thus frustrate their own best efforts.

Are you a rebel?

When we hurt ourselves, we are often attempting to hurt someone else as well. As children, often the only power we have—if we want to show our anger or frustration at feeling unloved or overlooked—is to disappoint parental expectations: We may do nothing, or refuse to do what we're told, sometimes throwing tantrums or being defiant in other ways, particularly during adolescence.

Anger directed against authority figures often derives from what we were told we *had* to do to please our parents—and we then do the opposite. This kind of behavior is very destructive because, in our effort to hurt and anger another person, we may give up the things we dearly love. If your parents wanted nothing more than for you to become a doctor, you may, despite your obvious talent in that direction, "choose" something different in order to shock or hurt them—or do nothing at all.

Ruin the fun for everyone
In your determination to hurt another person, you may sabotage a shared activity, such as going to the cinema, and end up feeling hurt and deprived yourself.

Understanding is the key

If you give up or refuse to do things that fulfill you in order to punish someone else, you will only succeed in hurting yourself. You need to become aware that you're losing something of immense value to yourself, and then think about how you can change your behavior. Once you understand why you act in this way, you can consciously choose what to do, rather than being driven by impulses that may work against you and against your potential.

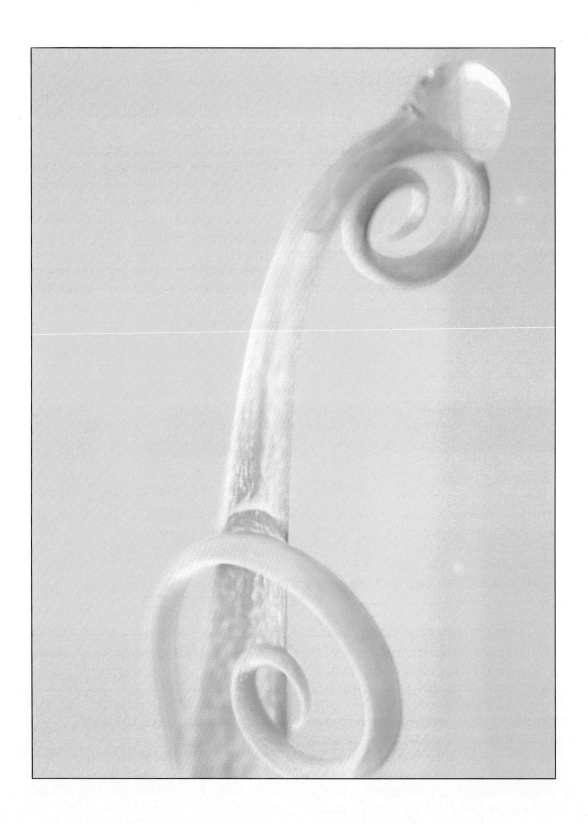

CHAPTER FIVE

GET GROWING!

AS YOU TAKE YOUR FIRST STEPS toward personal growth, you'll start to realize just how great your potential is and how much life has to offer. This chapter will help you stay on track, or give you a boost if you feel your enthusiasm waning.

If you're feeling frustrated, it can be tempting to make a sudden, drastic change in order to express the real you. It's wise to temper this feeling, however, with a more systematic approach. Devising a coherent plan, and considering possible outcomes before you make your move, will increase your chances of success (see "Thinking it Through," pp. 114-115). Once you have implemented a change, you may sometimes feel daunted or even disappointed. "Seeing it Through," pages 118-119, is a source of several tips for staying positive, enthusiastic, and committed—and thus in the best shape to achieve your goals.

One of the most effective ways to further growth is to create a challenge (see pp. 120-121). Trying something that stretches you beyond your comfort zone will develop your skills and strengths, and each success you achieve this way will bolster your self-confidence. When you are thinking of making changes or trying something new, you may fear the unpredictability of an unknown situation. "Take a Leap of Faith," pages 122-123, points out that, while there are no guarantees of success, sometimes you simply have to be brave, trust your judgment, and pursue your goal with wholehearted enthusiasm.

Some people find it hard to spend time alone because they associate it with loneliness and isolation. Solitude, however, yields rich rewards. It helps you reflect on your inner life, deepen your self-knowledge, and improve your relationships (see "Find a Quiet Place," pp. 126-127). Sometimes, a proper break may be what you need if you are feeling exhausted, overstressed, or in need of a respite from the demands of everyday life. Don't be too hard on yourself; accept that you sometimes need to take time out (see "Getting Away," pp. 128-129). A change is as good as a rest, and a course or retreat may help you clarify your aims, expand your horizons, or explore your inner self and spiritual life (see "Courses and Retreats," pp. 130-131).

There is no limit to how far you can travel on your own journey of growth. "Where Do I Go from Here?" pages 134-135, looks at the next steps you might choose to take, and at how much more you stand to gain once you realize just how much you can achieve.

IT'S TIME TO OPEN UP TO THE POSSIBILITIES OF A NEW LIFE AND

TO START GROWING IN THE DIRECTION YOU WANT.

COURAGE AND COMMITMENT WILL SEE YOU THROUGH.

THINKING IT THROUGH

A LL TOO OFTEN, if you're bored and restless with the present, the chances are you'll rush into decisions without considering the consequences. When a job is dull, a relationship seems stale, or you're discontented with your routine, it's easy to become impatient and want to throw yourself into something new in order to escape your frustration. Although it can seem easier to take immediate action rather than looking deeper into yourself to find the cause of your restlessness, if you don't think your choices through, you're far less likely to be content with the outcome. The result of hastiness can turn out to be simply an alternative to the present, rather than an improvement. A different job, for example, might seem to be an exciting new start, but if you have chosen it purely because of dissatisfaction with your current situation, it may be a step sideways instead of a step forward.

Understand your fears
Every day, you continually make choices, from trivial day-to-day matters to those that will alter your life considerably. But because any change introduces uncertainty, you may be indecisive or reluctant to initiate it until you're forced to by circumstances. Sometimes, you may act on impulse, grasping the first opportunity that comes along; at other times, you may hesitate and then find that you've missed the boat. You need to have the courage to confront your fears, and to understand why you need to make a change.

Approach things systematically
While we all have "instincts"—intuitive hunches—that help us to discover what we want out of life or which path to choose, we may lack the confidence to trust them, or be unsure about how to channel our desire for change. By combining instinct with a more systematic approach to implementing change, we can learn to make changes that are both constructive and rewarding. Firstly, it is crucial to consider all your options, and then set out your aims clearly. Making instant choices may appear decisive, but it can be foolhardy to dive blindly into the unknown. A little research, careful thought, and patience can help to make the future seem less daunting, and will help you see how you can realize your goals. It is also important to take time to look at the long-term

Choose the right path
There may be several ways to get where you want to go. Think carefully about which path will best help you to achieve your dream—it may not be the most direct route!

MAKING A DECISION

The first step to thinking an idea through is to confront all aspects of the need for change—the opportunities and benefits as well as the risks. The following points will help you to do this:

• **Clarify your aims**. Confront your current situation as objectively as you can. Ask yourself why you aren't happy with how things are. What do you need to change in order to improve them? Try to be specific.

• **Understand your motives**. Think about the reasons for your choice. Are you considering studying a subject simply because your family thinks you should? If you let yourself be swayed by others, you're less likely to be fulfilled by what you do.

• **Do your research**. Even if you trust your hunches, you still need to find out as much as you can about any proposed change.

• **Talk to people**. Discuss your ideas with people who have made similar choices, and be open to—but not swayed by—their opinions. Try to get a balanced view.

• **Write things down**. Take some time to write down the pros and cons of your decision. For example, a new job may mean more money but longer hours; would you willingly give up socializing with friends and family?

• **Assess the results**. Work out both what you *want* to gain and what you are *likely* to gain. What will be the immediate effects of your decision? And what will be the long-term effects? How will it affect both you and others?

• **Help yourself**. Try not to make important decisions when you're tired, emotional, or feeling pressured, as this is bound to affect your judgment.

implications of your decision to initiate change. This is something that Emma neglected to do when she became depressed by her mundane nine-to-five job. She resigned on the spur of the moment to take a full-time art course. At first, it seemed like an exciting move, but a few months into the course she was very unhappy. She could not afford to pay her rent, let alone go out, and her financial worries were affecting her studies. Emma also discovered that, despite her talent, she had to work extremely hard to complete challenging projects. She recognized that she had been unrealistic and hasty, and had neither the dedication nor the ability to complete the course—and felt more trapped and defeated than she had when working.

Jane, however, made a similar decision with very successful results. She had always wanted to get involved in radio production, but waited until she had earned enough money to see her through a one-year course. Before beginning, Jane talked to tutors, students, and her family, who provided her with helpful information as well as a wide range of opinions and advice. Having weighed everything up, she still was determined to do the course, but recognized that she would need to work in a bar two nights a week to cover her living costs. Thinking that she would only have to struggle for one year, she decided to proceed with her plan.

Mapping your journey

If you always stick to the familiar or more predictable path through life, you could miss valuable opportunities to learn or grow, or the chance to do something exciting and challenging—but you still need to think carefully about the path you take toward your goal. Bear in mind that taking the wrong path will not only waste time but will also undermine your confidence. You should be prepared for obstacles along the way, but by thinking your plan through and trying to anticipate difficulties, you will make your journey very much easier. Remember, too, that difficulties don't have to be excuses for not taking a new direction: If you come up with a practical plan for your intended change, you can accomplish almost anything.

TELLING OTHERS

After you've made a decision about a change you want to make, and have come up with a systematic and workable plan, you then need to tell other people; otherwise, your dream might simply remain in your head and never see the light of day. Many people find this is a difficult step, but instead of being afraid or hesitant about telling other people about your plans, you should consider that doing so is a major step toward realizing them—and that both you and others may benefit from your decision. Martin Luther King is a prime example of how communicating the need for change can move and enlist the support of others: He shared his vision of a society free from racism in passionate speeches that inspired his audiences so that many joined to help him achieve his dream.

Spread the word
Try to communicate any plans you have for change to the people in your life. It allows them to support your decision, and to feel involved rather than left behind.

Put it in writing
You might write down what you hope to achieve, and pin up what you've written on a bulletin board so that you can remind yourself of your goal every day. Another useful technique is to use what you've written as the basis for a letter you send to people, explaining your goals and plans in a way that doesn't make them feel excluded or frightened of your intentions.

Say it out loud
Even more powerful than a letter, however, is to communicate your resolution in person. Declaring your commitment in public can be daunting because your resolve will almost certainly be tested by the responses of other people. Bear in mind, however, that they may be happy and willing to support you, not simply ready to criticize you. If you communicate your idea in a way that excites others, they are more than likely to ask you how they can help; they may also be more willing than you would imagine to offer helpful advice or the names of people who might assist you.

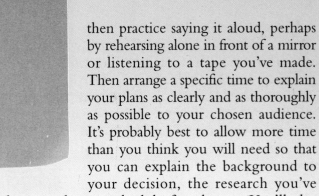

Who should you tell?

If you're making a far-reaching or life-changing decision, it will probably affect the people with whom you share your life, so the sooner you can involve them in your plans, the better. You should also tell anyone who might be able to help and support you when the going gets tough.

How should you tell them?

Any change you make can be very threatening to those closest to you, so it's wise to be careful how you tell them of your plans. The least successful way to initiate change is to be defiant of someone else's expectations, and accuse them of holding you back. They will become defensive, and may also feel saddened or angry that you view them in such a negative light. You may then feel guilty about your behavior as well as isolated and without support—feelings that will result in stagnation and stalemate rather than in growth and self-fulfillment.

• **Plan what you're going to say.** Try to have a clear picture of the "new" you, and let others know how positive this change will be. If you've been very morose, they will almost certainly benefit from a change that will make you happier and easier to live with. Refer to what you've written down,

then practice saying it aloud, perhaps by rehearsing alone in front of a mirror or listening to a tape you've made. Then arrange a specific time to explain your plans as clearly and as thoroughly as possible to your chosen audience. It's probably best to allow more time than you think you will need so that you can explain the background to your decision, the research you've done, and your schedule for change. You'll also want time to hear their views.

• **Practice with a friend.** Find someone with whom you can rehearse your side of the conversation, and ask for feedback about how you come across. If he or she knows the person with whom you intend to have a "real" conservation, ask your friend's opinion about the possible reactions you might get—or ask him or her to act like that person. Together you'll probably be able to anticipate their responses, and plan more helpful approaches.

• **Anticipate responses.** Realize that others might be surprised or even shocked by what you have to tell them, especially if they have had no idea how you've been feeling. Allow them some time to come to terms with your new ideas, and let them ask questions. The more you can reassure them that they are not part of any problem you're trying to solve, the more likely it is that they will support you.

All these preparations will pay great dividends, for with the support and good will of others, your goals will become very much easier to achieve.

SEEING IT THROUGH

When it comes to committing yourself to action, you may still feel overwhelmed by self-doubt, even if you've carefully considered your decision—all of a sudden your plans might seem over-ambitious. Facing the first day of a new job, for example, is very different from the relief at leaving an old one. How can you overcome your anxiety and follow through with your plans?

Convince yourself

Many people start off with great enthusiasm for an idea, yet lose interest before they can see it through. Perhaps they begin to feel ambivalent about a project, paralyzed by the fear of failure or the fear of success (see pp. 92-95). It may also be difficult to maintain a conviction about a particular course of action in the face of time pressures, stress, and other people's opinions.

If you feel any of these emotions, remind yourself of the ways your choices will make you happy, listen to your instincts, and trust your judgment and abilities. While you need to be decisive, you also need to be flexible, so revise your plans when necessary; don't stick with something because you feel you should in order to save face with others, or because you have invested time, money, and effort. There is always an alternative path.

Jack, for example, felt increasingly trapped as his wedding day drew closer. Most of his friends tried to convince him that he was suffering typical pre-wedding nerves, but Jack increasingly felt he was going through with the wedding for the wrong reasons—mainly because he and his fiancée were thought by everyone to be the "perfect" couple, and he felt he had to please her as well as his parents. He also thought he had to stabilize his stressful professional life as a journalist. Guilty about the time and money spent preparing for the occasion, he feared letting everyone down. Finally, a good friend sat him down and made him ask himself the following question: "Is this choice likely to bring me long-term happiness?" Jack realized that going through with the ceremony would only lead to regret and resentment in

the future, that he felt too unsettled to commit himself to family life, and so, three months before the wedding, he reluctantly broke off the engagement. He disappointed several people, but he made what he felt was the right decision.

Don't give up!

If you feel overwhelmed by a task you've set for yourself, keep your long-term goal in sight—it will help you see your ideas through—and pay attention to each step along the way.

Stay focused

If you find yourself vacillating or "losing steam," focus on the rewards your decision will bring. For example, if you want to run a marathon, think of the health benefits, make a date by which you want to achieve your goal so that you have something concrete to work toward, and reward yourself for any progress you make, perhaps by treating yourself to a new pair of running shoes when you achieve a faster time for a specific distance. It's also important not to focus on your weaknesses or on what you could have done better. Don't be put off by previous failures—either your own or those of other people. Instead, tell yourself that you have the strength of mind needed for commitment, and that this is your chance to succeed.

MAKE IT HAPPEN

Spur yourself on by believing in yourself and making the most of your opportunities. These points will help to keep you on the right track.
• **Take the initiative.** Don't be afraid to *make* things happen—and don't make excuses for not trying.
• **Look ahead.** Don't be put off if you've made bad choices in the past, or if your first steps toward your new goal are uncertain or unsuccessful. Take the long view, and remind yourself of what you want.
• **Give it your best shot.** If you've made up your mind to do something, don't be half-hearted or too tentative—give yourself the best chance of making it work.
• **Stay positive.** There can be a sense of anticlimax after an important decision is made, or disappointments or failures occur. A new job, for example, may quickly become routine. Even when things don't turn out as you would like, being decisive and taking action are still positive steps toward personal fulfillment.

CREATE A CHALLENGE

ANY DECISION to grow or change may seem so intimidating that it may be very hard to get started. The solution is to break down the goal into a series of simple objectives, and start to stretch yourself. The benefit of such an approach is that each challenge is easier to achieve on its own, and with each achievement, your confidence and self-esteem grow. If you were going to learn to swim, for example, you wouldn't expect to jump into the deep end and start from there. It's the same with personal growth: It takes time. You need to approach the shallow end of the pool from the steps and begin to feel confident in the water before you think about swimming. Once you've tackled one challenge in this way, you'll probably be much less afraid to take on bigger challenges in the future.

Getting beyond the comfort zone

Why is the first step toward a new objective so hard? Probably because each of us has a "comfort zone" of familiar, tried-and-true behavior that makes us feel secure. Even if you're frustrated and know you're stuck in a rut, it's still difficult to imagine that your future can be different.

You should begin your journey of personal growth by creating a challenge that takes you beyond the comfort zone of what you would normally do. Even simple changes of routine will encourage you to be more imaginative and take bigger risks. Examples of things you can do to prepare yourself for change are taking on new tasks at work, or reserving one night a week to read instead of watching television. While you perform each new activity, be aware of your feelings: Are you anxious, or do you feel excited and enthusiastic?

Enjoy the thrill

One of the reasons that people change their lives, often trying something they've never done before simply for the thrill of it, is out of a need for novelty and stimulation. The advantage of making changes in your life is that the world starts to look different—and this can be very enjoyable. Think of something you would never normally do because you're afraid of making a fool of yourself—then consider doing it! You could try roller-blading, a dance class, or learning about computers. Challenges don't need to be serious all the time, or have a serious purpose; in fact, trying something simply for the fun of it is important for two reasons: Firstly, it is a great way to stretch yourself, and get used to the idea that you can be different. Secondly, you might discover that change is exhilarating rather than frightening. Released from your inhibitions, you'll probably feel a surge of enthusiasm and vitality, and feel more alive as a result. Heartened by all these feelings, you might then find that you can't wait to face your next challenge.

Stretch yourself
Any new challenge is like learning to swim. First, you have to stretch yourself beyond your comfort zone. Then, instead of jumping in at the deep end, you should pace yourself, and work toward simple, achievable objectives.

DO IT NOW!

The points below will help you to get to grips with a challenge you have set yourself.

1. Get started. Take the first step as soon as possible. Once you've started, it's easier to continue. The more you procrastinate, the less motivated you'll be.

2. Keep it simple. By creating simple, easily achievable steps, your goal will seem more manageable instead of an impossible dream.

3. Create a structure. Set aside a specific time to devote yourself to your goal. Buy the tools or equipment you need, and find the best environment in which to work.

4. Review your progress. Keep track of your progress by creating a timetable or keeping a diary in which to record your thoughts about what you're doing.

5. Keep your goal in mind. To inspire yourself, create reminders of what you want to achieve: If you want to learn French, for example, you could put up pictures or postcards of France at work or in your study.

6. Keep at it. Consistent application will help you achieve your goal sooner, and is psychologically more rewarding than the occasional burst of frantic effort.

7. Find someone to support you. Someone with experience in the area you're interested in, or simply a friend or classmate, can encourage you by offering helpful advice and asking how you're getting on.

8. Celebrate every achievement. Each and every small step on the way to your objective should be a source of pride—and a reminder that you can be a new person.

TAKE A LEAP OF FAITH

Personal growth involves taking leaps of faith. It means moving into areas where you cannot be completely confident of success, where your experience is limited, and where only faith can give you the impetus to proceed. Do you remember how you felt on the day you started school, moved away from home, or started a new job? You may have been excited, looked forward to new experiences, and made plans. In the case of a promotion, you probably worked hard to develop your skills, and were over-joyed to be given recognition, a higher salary, and new responsibilities. Then, on the morning of the big day, it was all rather different. Fears of how you might cope, and the realization of just how different life would become, bubbled to the surface, and you probably felt like hiding, or looked for ways to avoid taking the big step.

Understand your fears

It is important to recognize and under-stand that fear is a natural response to the unknown. New experiences are often perceived as dangerous because we have no way of knowing whether we're going to flourish in the new circumstances.

It is extraordinary how concerned we feel about new stages in our lives when, in fact, our real-life experience of past new beginnings is usually quite positive and exhilarating. It would be safe to assume that you survived each and every one of the new beginnings you've had, and probably are grateful that you took each step. As a way of coping with anxiety about the future, try listing all the new experiences and significant milestones you've been through in your life. These might include leaving home, your first day at college, starting your first job, getting married, or having children. For each experience, think back to how you felt when the decisive moment actually came, and how you feel about it now.

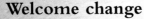

Welcome change

If you're nervous about a big decision, remind yourself of the reasons you decided to embark on a journey of personal growth. There was probably something frustrating about the way you were living or you wouldn't have wanted to change things. Perhaps you simply need to remind yourself that you're more than capable of facing the unknown, just as you did with all the other major steps you've taken in your life. Tell yourself that you can face the challenges and the lessons to be learned, and recognize that new situations bring possibilities for life to be better, more exciting, and more satisfying.

Seek inspiration from others

There are many inspiring examples of people who have taken enormous steps to change their lives and have succeeded. Some are world-famous, such as the rock star Sting, who gave up a career in teaching to try his luck in the music business. Many big businesses, too, started from modest beginnings. Success is not simply about fame and fortune, however. Linda, for example, was a successful solicitor when she decided to change her life shortly after the birth of her first child. Her leap of faith was to resign her partnership. Five years later, she has new skills and a variety of freelance jobs. Because she works for herself, she decides which projects she will or will not take on, and is able to spend more time with her children. Satisfied with her working life and less stressed, all her relationships—especially her marriage—are a greater source of fulfillment. Her calculated risk reaped great benefits.

Tony, too, took an enormous leap of faith when he decided to move from England to Holland. He had Dutch friends who offered him an exciting job, an idea that immediately appealed to him: The job meant more responsibility, and he loved Amsterdam. His excitement was short-lived, however, when he realized the implications of such a move. He would have to sell or rent out his house, give up the security of his present job, leave behind his family and friends, and learn a new language.

For about two weeks Tony wavered between fear and exhilaration. Slowly, however, he began to put things into perspective. Because he would already have a job and friends, he realized it would be relatively easy for him to fit in. Nor would he be under great pressure to learn Dutch right away because it was not necessary for his job and many Dutch people speak English. Tony also knew that the distance between England and Holland was not so great that he could not keep in contact with his family and friends. He decided that the risks were worth taking, made the move to Holland, and is convinced it was the best decision of his life.

The danger in not taking a leap into the unknown is that you may find yourself trapped in an unsatisfying life. Instead, resolve to be brave, start planning, and prepare to leap into the new life that will be perfect for the new you.

Enjoy the stretch
Making any big change is like moving to a new country: Everything will be strange but also exciting, stretching you in new or unforeseen ways.

STAYING THE COURSE

What happens after you've taken the first steps toward your goal, only to find yourself stuck despite your best efforts? Perhaps you still can't have a conversation in the language you're struggling to learn, or your boss hasn't recognized how you've really been making an effort to contribute to the weekly meeting, or you're still not allowed to answer the telephones at the helpline where you've been training as a volunteer. You probably feel very frustrated and disheartened, but you should try to remember that some changes take a long time to implement. What can you do to help yourself through a slow or difficult stage?

Identify the problem

Start by reviewing what you're doing and how you're approaching it. Firstly, check that you're still committed to achieving your goals. Sometimes it is possible to get carried away and devise too many challenges, only to find that some of them are not what you really want. If you're ambivalent about your goals, you'll find it very difficult to keep going. But, if you *are* still committed and you are not having any success, consider your strategies.

Lisa, for example, had decided to live and work abroad for two reasons: she felt it would be a beneficial career move, and also thought she would enjoy the challenge of a completely new environment. Although she had spent months arranging with her company to work for three years in Paris, she found she was not as happy as she expected to be. After a year, she was very lonely, daunted by the language barrier, and was not sure she would be able to complete her agreed contract. Finally, she asked a colleague at work what she could do, and discovered that there were several groups she could join through her country's embassy, ranging from sports teams to intensive language groups and art appreciation societies. As a result, Lisa found a whole new circle of friends with whom she spent an enriching time.

Keep the end in sight
Unless you remain committed to your goals, you might become disheartened by the hurdles that will inevitably confront you along the way.

Learn as you grow

You may have set your heart on a goal that you can attain relatively quickly, such as learning how to type, or something that takes a great deal longer to develop, such as speaking a foreign language fluently. Whichever it is, keep the following points in mind:

• **Review your activities.** Recognize all the positive steps—however small—that you've taken to reach your goal. Try to ascertain which steps were successful, and why. Give yourself credit for responding creatively to problems, and for having the ingenuity to create new options when you have a setback, especially one that is unexpected.

• **Be flexible.** Adapt your stategies and try new approaches. Don't blame yourself for unforeseen circumstances that are beyond your control, but that might contribute to a feeling that you're getting nowhere fast. Don't be tempted to give up at this point. Instead, accept that you're bound to feel clumsy when you start anything new, and will most likely stumble, but that you can decide to get back on your feet.

• **Ask for feedback.** Other people might recognize your achievements more easily than you do, and will be happy to help keep up your morale when your confidence or enthusiasm wanes. Try to be gracious in accepting well-meant advice; it's not meant to undermine your confidence.

• **Be inspired.** Remember that growth is endless, and that once you meet your objectives, you'll almost certainly decide to set yourself new challenges in order to develop further.

ENCOURAGE YOURSELF

It can be very difficult to believe in yourself when the going gets tough, and your goal seems to vanish before your eyes. One way to maintain your confidence is to recognize that you will make mistakes—so you should allow yourself a certain margin of error, and recognize that very few mistakes are irrevocable. If you're a perfectionist, you may have to learn to be kind to yourself, and not to criticize yourself too harshly for not achieving every target. One way you can do this is to pamper yourself after a setback to revive your self-esteem. Make a list of possible rewards or treats—such as buying a jacket that makes you feel great, having a massage, playing a game of golf, taking a walk in the country—and when you feel discouraged, choose something from your list.

Occasionally treating and pampering yourself is an important part of personal growth. It will remind you that growth is not simply about achieving your goal, but is also about *how* you change, and how you acknowledge yourself for your own efforts, during your journey toward greater fulfillment. Finally, remember that failure is not what happens when you fall down—it's when you don't get up again.

Don't give up
If you feel that you're still a long way from hitting your target, don't resort to relentless self-criticism—this will only set you back even further. Just learn from your mistakes and try again!

FIND A QUIET PLACE

FOR MANY OF US, life is a frenzied whirl of activity, noise, color, and high-tech gadgetry that makes endless demands on our time and energy. We tend to envy the person who is successful in both his or her social life and career, who has clear goals, and who is constantly striving to meet professional and personal targets. However, what we often overlook is that such accomplishments, based on a carefully wrought and packed agenda, may add up to an impressive and dauntingly efficient lifestyle, but could also leave little time for appreciating the joys of solitude, those moments of quiet introspection so essential for replenishing physical and emotional needs.

Alone or lonely?

The main reason we fear solitude is because we confuse it with isolation and loneliness. Sometimes, people are isolated because they are out of work, have lost a partner, or have moved away from family and friends. In this case, they are on their own not out of choice but because of an unwanted or unforeseen change of circumstances. It's also possible to feel lonely because you can't express who you really are, and are surrounded by people with whom you can't really communicate. Solitude, however, is completely different. For one thing, many people *choose* solitude: They thrive in their own company because they need to collect their own thoughts or pursue a special project without distractions. Most people who deliberately seek solitude do so in order to "recharge their batteries." Without such quiet interludes, they may feel that they are losing touch with their inner life—forfeiting the chance to feel serene, to explore their thoughts and feelings, or to plan for the future.

You may be afraid that, by seeking solitude, you'll be hiding yourself away from what might be enjoyable or beneficial company. Some people, however, shy away from solitude for other, less obvious reasons. A busy schedule can be a way of hiding feelings or parts of yourself that you find difficult to accept, such as feelings of emptiness (see "Addicted to Action," pp. 100–101). Perhaps you're afraid that time on your own will be spent in dwelling obsessively on your faults, past mistakes, or current problems. This is not necessarily so: Solitude may allow you the opportunity to understand yourself better so that you make fewer mistakes. If you do tend to slip into obsessional thinking, however, try a little creative visualization: You might imagine something you regret having said or done as a vivid stain on a piece of material; now picture it gradually fading away in bright sunlight until it disappears. Such mental exercises are a good way to envision a brighter future for yourself, and are most effective if you do them on your own.

The search for solitude

You might well say, "OK, I know I need solitude, but I have a partner, three children, and a demanding job. Surely all of these must come first?" The answer is that unless you nourish your inner being, you can't possibly give your best to the people and tasks in your life; some time alone is the very least that you deserve. We benefit from solitude in our lives: time to reflect on who we are, to re-establish a relationship with our inner self, and to consider our role in the outside world. Solitude is thus the foundation of our relationships with others. In her *Intimacy and Solitude Self-Therapy Book*, psychotherapist Stephanie Dowrick writes: "Your capacity for solitude, for feeling comfortable when alone with your own self, exists on a continuum with your capacity for intimacy—being in good contact with others." Making time for yourself will allow you to get to know yourself, and to develop all your talents and strengths. You'll discover what your emotional needs and expectations are, what you contribute to relationships, and what you appreciate about other people. Your relationships will be enriched because time spent with other people will feel more like an active choice, instead of simply a habit or duty. Because you have time to reflect on the reasons why relationships sometimes go wrong, solitude can also heal the petty resentments that can build up between you and another person. For all these reasons, you should never be afraid to ask those around you for some time alone; they will soon discover that this improves, rather than damages, your relationship.

Think of an oasis

The fact that increasing numbers of people are choosing to take time out at "retreats" of some sort, which may or may not be religious, and where they can contemplate their spiritual or inner selves in peace, is an indication of just how powerful our need for quiet contemplation is. Such solitude is, Stephanie Dowrick believes, "a unique source of joy, knowledge, ease, and strength"—so create an oasis of calm in your busy life, a place from which you can see more clearly the next step on your path of personal growth.

TAKE YOUR TIME

Depending on your lifestyle, there are many different ways in which you can make room for solitude. Make time in your schedule, and consider doing any of the following things:
• Go for regular, short walks on your own.
• Get up a little earlier, or stay up later, than others you live with.
• Take a long soak in the bath, perhaps by the light of scented candles.
• Look out of your window for five minutes and concentrate on some beautifully shaped clouds overhead, or a spectacular sunset.
• Sit down for a short while and listen to some soothing music. You might have to do this when everyone else is asleep or out, or perhaps you can "switch off" sufficiently by using headphones.
• Take five minutes out while you're sitting on the bus or doing some mundane task to conjure up a relaxing visualization: Imagine yourself drifting slowly down a river in an open boat or dancing barefoot in a flower-filled meadow.
• Take a few hours off—don't listen to the radio, don't watch television, and take the telephone off the hook. Listen to the sounds of silence.
• Go and stay in the country for a few days and enjoy long, contemplative walks alone.
• Attend a short residential course of some kind—alone (see pp. 130-131).

Where are you headed?
A solitary walk in peaceful surroundings will help you stay in touch with your inner self and clarify long-term goals..

GETTING AWAY

Whenever we are going through periods of enormous strain, most of us are much too hard on ourselves, thinking we have to soldier on no matter what. This is hardly surprising, considering that most Western societies are based on the values of a goal-oriented work ethic. These values also foster a rather puritanical streak, making many people feel frightened and anxious about admitting that they can't cope, have to take time off, or need occasionally to enjoy themselves for the sake of it.

Somehow, we may feel that, unless we are suffering in some way, what we are doing cannot possibly be "worthwhile." We feel guilty whenever we find a way of stepping off this treadmill, and try to justify it to ourselves and to everyone around us.

A great escape?

Instead of forcing yourself to go on, try giving in for a change: If you feel a strong urge to spend the weekend in bed, or take a little time off, then do it—your mind and body may be telling you that you need it. You probably know only too well that, on occasions, taking some time out and putting a little geographical and psychological distance between yourself and a problem can work wonders. This might just mean a couple of days away, reading and going for walks; it might mean moving to another part of the country and starting a new life; it could be a six-month round-the-world trip.

If you judge it correctly, getting away—having a suitable break when you really need it—can be a real life-saver. Often, it is only when you are away from your everyday surroundings and in a relaxed environment that you can start to work through your problems objectively and effectively. Judge it incorrectly, however, and you could create a whole new set of problems.

TELL-TALE SIGNS

How can you tell if you need to get away? If things have got on top of you, you may suffer regularly from any of the following:
• Constant, pent-up anxiety or restlessness
• Breathlessness, heart palpitations, dizziness, bowel upsets, headaches, aches and pains, and nausea that seem to have no cause
• A growing dependency on alcohol or drugs of any sort, including cigarettes
• Great increase or decrease in your appetite
• Insomnia or nightmares
• Panic attacks and phobias
• Constant exhaustion
• Allergies
• Nervous mannerisms

You may be feeling mild anxiety, and a short break might be all you need. For example, you might be working hard on a difficult project and feeling the strain. You could perhaps nip this in the bud by streamlining your routine, delegating where you can, going to bed earlier, giving yourself treats—and by making sure that you enjoy yourself whenever you can.

A world apart …
Sometimes you have to get away from it all so that you can unwind and see yourself and your life from a different perspective.

Making the right break

When is getting away for some peace simply "getting away from it all," and when is it running away from reality? Mark was stunned when his girlfriend of ten years suddenly left him. Friends suggested that he stay with them for a while, or go away for a short break, but Mark felt that this would be "weak." He threw himself into his work until he felt he was at breaking point, then he handed in his notice and left to travel around Europe for a few months. This was one of the bleakest times of his life—obsessively chewing over the past and worrying about how he would cope financially when he went home, he felt aimless, friendless, and disorientated. When he finally returned, the problems from which he had tried to flee were still staring him in the face.

When something dramatic has happened to you, it can feel as though you have to redress the balance equally dramatically by getting as far away as possible. In fact, the last thing you probably need is to find yourself in a totally strange environment; familiar routines and surroundings can provide the comfort and stability you sorely need to gain perspective. Give yourself time to adjust to a new situation, perhaps taking a short holiday to think things over. Then, some months later, when you're feeling stronger and more settled, and your priorities are clearer, you can still make a complete change.

Take time out

If you suffer from certain tell-tale signs of overdoing things (see box, left), you must start to take time out now, and use it wisely. If you do manage to take a day off, don't use it to catch up on chores and errands, or to visit a relative with whom you have never really got along. If you can't take time off, start by having a few relaxing evenings or early nights; keep a journal of how you're feeling and monitor your progress. If you still feel stressed after a week or two of taking it easy, you might want to go away for a weekend. If your symptoms persist, it may be time to consider having a much longer, complete break of some sort (see pp. 130-131).

Rather than being tough on yourself for not working hard enough, try being tough on yourself for *not* taking enough time out. All it takes is a little shift in your thinking. Make that little voice inside your head say, "Have you had a really good break recently?" instead of "Couldn't you work just that little bit harder?" Have signs or notes with the former message on stuck up around your home or office. Make firm arrangements to do things that would be difficult or costly to get out of—such as paying for travel tickets well in advance—or enlist the support of a friend with whom to relax. Learn to recognize what getting away can do for you, and make proper time and space for it in your life.

COURSES AND RETREATS

Do you need to get back on track in your journey of personal growth, or want a boost to help you make changes? Or want to get away to reflect on your development or expand your horizons? If you'd like something more than an ordinary vacation, you might choose a personal development course or seminar for guidance and support. There are residential centers that cater for almost every possible kind of quest for personal growth—from weekend courses aimed at developing your creativity, to a few days spent in silent meditation at a monastery.

What do you want?

To help you choose the right place for you, ask yourself exactly how you hope to benefit from your time away, and find out all you can about the center before you book. The kinds of benefit a center or course will offer fall into four main categories, and you can expect to be doing the following things:

1. Developing or exploring a specific skill, such as painting or rock-climbing, or learning about a particular subject. You may be coming to a subject for the first time, or building on a long-standing interest.

2. Meeting people who either share similar interests, or who will introduce you to different ways of looking at things—both of which can be highly rewarding and stimulating experiences. A course might offer the chance to enhance your ability to work with others, especially as part of a team.

3. Getting away from the bustle of life to a place where you can find complete peace and rest.

4. Exploring a specific aspect of yourself and your personal development.

What will you get?

Many centers cater for all of these interests and needs, some for just one or two. There may be many lectures and workshops, or nothing to do except rest and reflect on your life. Many will be in large country houses or in attractive surroundings that will lift your spirits and provide the opportunity for enjoyable, contemplative walks. Meals are often eaten communally, and centers may cater for special diets. You may be able to go for a day, a weekend, a week or two, or several months. If the center is a whole community, then there may be the option to join them on a more long-term basis.

What will you learn?

What such centers offer can be put into broad groups, as follows:

• **Hobby courses,** such as painting, writing, making jewelry, or learning an instrument are quite popular. There are also residential courses that aim to explore your general creativity, allowing you to feel uninhibited about singing and dancing, for example, even if you feel that you have no talent for these things (see "But I Can't Draw!" pp. 54–55). These courses may be ideal if you want to express yourself more freely and develop your creativity.

• **Outdoor and activity courses** may have a broader agenda than you think. Outward Bound, which runs all kinds of outdoor courses, was founded by Kurt Hahn, who believed that facing physical challenges also helped us face unknown parts of ourselves, our strengths and weaknesses. These courses can help you understand yourself, and how you interact with others and approach challenges.

Many people find that outdoor activities provide the chance to feel in tune with nature. This uplifting experience can be enhanced by the satisfaction of pitting yourself and your physical skills against the elements. It may also help you develop your capacity to work as part of a team. In fact, many companies now send their employees on outdoor courses, which are sometimes extremely gruelling, to test their real mettle and assess their leadership qualities.

• **Centers aimed at nourishing spiritual life** come in every form imaginable. Many are tied strictly to a specific religion, although visitors do not always have to be a follower of that faith. Some monasteries and convents now offer anyone the chance to spend a few peaceful days in their midst. Others are entirely non-denominational, with a spiritual emphasis but no element of organized religion. Some might expect you to join in the daily routine of chores and prayers; others may leave you to do as you wish. There may be a rule of silence, or the community might be bustling and busy; some offer a range of activities, perhaps on a theme such as gardening or music, during which you can enjoy talking to lots of very different people. You may be welcome as an individual or a family, or be required to go as part of a prearranged group.

Some centers and retreats have a spiritual counselor there to help out with any specific issues you might want to discuss, or offer guided study. It's up to you to find out what to expect before you go.

• **Personal growth centers** is a loose term that can be used to refer to the enormous range of courses that might also be put under the umbrella term "New Age." Many of these concentrate on a specific school of "alternative" thought, such as faith healing; others might offer a mix, for example, of yoga, meditation, and painting. Some are in inner cities, but most are in the country or located in such idyllic locations as the Greek islands.

Using your judgment

Many people worry that, on certain alternative or spiritual courses, efforts may be made to "brainwash" them or to recruit them to some strange sect. The rule of thumb here is that this is by far the exception rather than the rule, but you should make every effort to discover what is being offered, and who sponsors the organization. Trust your feelings; if you are asked to do anything that makes you uncomfortable, don't do it—and this includes parting with large financial "donations." You are here to help yourself, after all, no-one else.

A quiet haven
Going on retreat or on a course can help you reflect on your inner life and your future development, test yourself, explore new experiences, or express your creativity.

GOING ALONE, GOING TOGETHER

WHATEVER ROUTE your personal, inner journey takes, one of the most important discoveries that you will make along the way is that the final responsibility for your development rests with you alone. You will never be completely happy until you're happy with yourself and with your own company, so you should try to view solitude as an enriching experience (see pp. 126-127).

It is just as true to say, however, that neither will you progress if you cut yourself off from other people. We all need people to give us a more objective view of what we're doing and where we're going in life, and talking to others gives us the warmth of human companionship, and the chance to enjoy shared views. Such an exchange also provides the chance to consider a completely different approach. In some cases, we need someone else's special expertise to help us out with certain problems. So how do you know where to draw your personal guidelines—when to deal with things on your own, and when to turn to others for help?

Your framework
Putting the elements of your life into perspective will give you a clearer idea of your ability to cope in different situations.

Building a personal framework

It is important to get the elements of your everyday life into some sort of perspective. This will give you a framework within which it should be clear whether you can rely on your own inner resources to get you through or would benefit from turning to others. Firstly, think about the small, day-to-day challenges that you face, such as being on time for an appointment or eating healthily, and consider how you deal with them. Now consider some of the larger problems that come your way, for example, how you cope with a difficult colleague.

Lastly, reflect on some of the major changes or crises in your life, and how you dealt with these. Record your feelings in a journal, and jot down any thoughts; then you can look back over it to see how you coped. When you're reviewing these situations, consider whether you managed fine on your own, or wished you had sought someone else's help. There are no hard and fast rules, but you should be able to make minor practical decisions in your life without asking for help. If you find that you have to ask for help or advice with a whole host of small matters, then you need to ask yourself why you have so little faith in your own abilities and judgment.

HELPING CHECKLIST

If you decide to seek outside help, make sure that you keep the following points in mind:
• Only stick with a course of action while it is really helping; don't be afraid to say no or to stop.
• Don't stop at the first source of help; explore different options until you find one that suits you. Give each one a real chance.
• One type of help will suit at one stage of a problem, while another type might be better at another stage. A combination of strategies or therapies might be appropriate at all stages.
• Don't become over-reliant on outside help—it is supposed to help you find your way, not create another problem by undermining your confidence or independence.
• Help should be a human, learning relationship for both parties, and both of you should work hard at the collaboration. The relationship should remain flexible and not become a vehicle for promoting the helper's sense of self-importance.
• *You*, not someone else, must make any final decisions about your life.

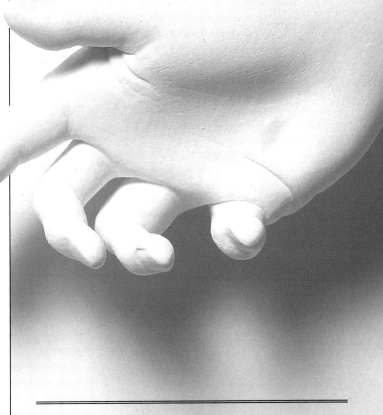

A helping hand?
As you grow, you may want to work through some changes on your own; at other times, you will want the support of others.

What does "help" mean?

Getting "help" means just that—whatever helps you. Again, you must assume personal responsibility for seeking out and accepting assistance; only you can determine what benefits you. You need to know whether you want a sympathetic shoulder to cry on, some factual information, or an exploration of your inner thought processes and feelings.

People who might help include a close friend or relative who is empathetic or has dealt with a similar experience, your partner, a phone helpline, a self-help group, a doctor, or a counselor. If you feel you'd like more specialist help for a more difficult or persistent problem, it will help to recall that, broadly speaking, there are two main types of therapy:

1. Directive: Here, you tend to be given specific things to do; for example, a behavior therapist might give someone who suffers from panic attacks specific techniques to use to reduce their anxiety.

2. Non-directive: A therapist would not tell you what you should do; rather, the emphasis is on unraveling what your feelings and experiences mean.

There are various professionals, such as:
• *Psychologists*, who tend to analyze behavior and mental processes within a wider social context.
• *Psychiatrists*, who may approach mental well-being from a more medical point of view.
• *Psychotherapists or counselors*, who may combine various elements to tailor a personal approach to your psychological and emotional well-being, or follow a particular set of beliefs.

These distinctions are simplistic, however, and there is often an overlap in both approach and the kind of help offered. As well as individual therapy, you can be seen with your partner, or in a group.

You may decide that you need a combination of helpers, or just one. You might initially ask a friend for help and then progress further when that isn't enough. Never be afraid to ask for help. The less afraid you are of asking for different kinds of help, the less dependent you are likely to become, provided that you recognize that any help you seek must be the means to an end: to enhance your own ability to make important decisions yourself.

WHERE DO I GO FROM HERE?

PERSONAL GROWTH is a lifelong journey, and once you embark on self-discovery, you'll soon find out that it is exciting to keep going. Having glimpsed what can be gained, you'll find it easier to motivate yourself; the changes you make will have a positive effect on other areas of your life, and your development will gather momentum.

As author Liz Hodgkinson says in her *Personal Growth Handbook*, this development is like decorating a house—once you get one room looking really good, then all the others seem grimy and dull by contrast, so you have to keep going! So, for example, once you find it easier to deal effectively with people who are close to you, you might want to look at how you relate to your work colleagues—or vice versa.

Taking off

Your journey of personal growth may have been prompted by any number of different situations. Perhaps you gradually came to realize that your life needed reviewing, or you had a blinding revelation one day that you were on the wrong path; perhaps a major crisis forced you to take a much harder look at yourself. You might have started the process entirely by yourself, or in tandem with a counselor of some sort. Reading this book might provide your initial spark. Whatever your personal story, one question will be very important: Where do I go from here? There is only one general way to answer this—keep going. If your journey began in therapy of some kind, you may feel that it is time for a spell of going it alone. Or perhaps you began by reading new books and articles, making an effort to talk to new people about different matters that interest you, or attending lectures and discussion groups. If so, the time may now be ripe for trying therapy if you still feel you have difficult issues that require the support of a trained counselor, or if there is a specific or temporary crisis for which you need constructive help. You might decide that you want to participate in a personal growth seminar or course.

The path of change

What you may well find is that, once you become more attuned to your inner life, the next step suggests itself naturally. Gail, for example, was someone who thought that all personal growth talk was nonsense. After years of being in a job she hated, she finally resigned. Shortly after this, she found that she was also able to stop overeating—something she had tried and failed to do many times. Soon, she found she was making great strides in her efforts to keep in touch with friends—only it wasn't such an effort any more. Gail realized that finding the strength to take control of her life had been the wellspring from which

A continuous journey
The journey of personal growth is a rich and varied one; how, and at what pace, you travel—and what course you take—are up to you.

other changes started to flow, but she felt she needed to make more sense of the changes in her life. She decided to do something she would never have considered just a few months previously: to see a therapist. Gail wanted to become more conscious of her inner life, and to consider where to go next. Just as she had seen a careers counselor to analyze her job skills and choose the right career path, Gail wanted to develop her life skills and commit herself to conscious and beneficial changes in the future.

Onward and upward

Just because there is always room for improvement doesn't mean you should judge yourself harshly. It should be exciting to realize that you have the capacity to grow and improve your life.

It's a good idea to review your progress regularly—keeping a journal is extremely helpful, and will also help you to overcome any fears you have about changing direction or exploring a new line of thought or therapy. Another technique you might try is to draw up a chart that divides your life into different spheres—work, home, leisure—then note your progress in each sphere. It's important to balance these three elements effectively; if, for example, you've concentrated on one particular area, ask yourself if it's time to switch to another. The whole point of personal growth is that you do just that—grow. It helps to remember that what suited you once won't suit you forever, nor should it.

Words of wisdom…

It's perfectly natural that, at any stage of your journey of personal growth, you may feel fainthearted or uncertain about what you're doing, why you're doing it, or where you're going. Such hesitation is understandable, but if you need encouragement to take the first step toward fulfilling your potential, bear in mind what Goethe, the great eighteenth-century German poet and playwright, wrote about initiative and creation: "Whatever you can do or dream you can, begin it now. Boldness has genius, power, and magic."

THE SEEDS OF GROWTH

DO YOU FEEL that you are really fulfilling your potential? Or are you convinced that life must have more to offer you? Personal growth, or personal development, is about understanding what you need in order to be who you really are or want to be—and then being able to take tangible steps toward achieving it. The journey of self-development may involve many ups and downs as you come to terms with loss and disappointment, move on from past hurts and limiting patterns of behavior, and explore undiscovered realms of your personality, talents, feelings, and immense capabilities. It is the journey of a lifetime.

Time to "be"
If you find it hard to sit still even for a moment, you may be using incessant activity as a way of blocking out uncomfortable feelings and realizations. Taking time out for mental and physical relaxation, or simply doing nothing, can help you get more in touch with your true needs.

Daydreams and fantasies
Your imagination is much more than a way to escape reality or withdraw from the demands of daily life. Your daydreams and fantasies can yield valuable insights into your inner desires and secret aspirations.

The "real" you
You cannot aim for what you want unless you know and understand the real you. For some people, this search for self-awareness may involve therapy or other professional guidance; for others, self-knowledge simply grows with time and maturity. Knowing yourself allows you to live and act in harmony with your inner needs, and so feel integrated and "whole."

The right time
Knowing when it's time to change—and having the courage to face the new and unknown— is a vital part of growth. We often feel safest with what is familiar and predictable, even if it's making us unhappy. By accepting that change is a fact of life, you can move beyond your existing limitations and develop your talents and awareness.

Goals and challenges
Your dreams and desires may inspire you, but they can also be a source of frustration if you never implement plans to bring them to fruition. Set yourself specific, concrete goals and divide them into stages. In this way, you won't feel overwhelmed by too great a challenge, and you can measure and enjoy your progress.

Your everyday life

Goals are important when you are committed to change, but do not let your long-term aims blind you to the abundant pleasures of your everyday life. Take the time to enjoy the journey of self-discovery, rather than rushing impatiently to your destination, and appreciate who you are and what you've already accomplished.

Other people

None of us exists in a vacuum. When you make changes to your life, it inevitably affects others, who may find the changes unsettling or even threatening. If you want the support of people close to you, take the time to communicate clearly about your intentions, and reassure them of your continued love for them.

Your spiritual needs

You don't have to subscribe to a particular religion to have a spiritual dimension to your life. Some people explore their spirituality through creative expression, some through meditation, some by going on retreats to find a sanctuary in which to explore their thoughts and feelings. Whatever route you choose, being in tune with your spiritual needs and "higher" self can be a source of great inner peace and enhanced self-knowledge.

Your work

Do you find your work rewarding and satisfying? Or is it simply a means of making money? If your work does not fulfill you, it may be time to think of changing direction, perhaps exploring a long-cherished dream or finding ways to use your existing job to make greater use of your potential.

Outside help

It is never an admission of weakness to seek help from others in your quest for personal growth. Many people find that talking about their feelings and uncertainties with a professional, such as a therapist or counselor, is an invaluable source of comfort and insight. There are many seminars and courses that can help you find a way forward.

SOLUTIONS

What's Your Attitude?
(pp. 22-25)

Before you embark on your journey of personal growth, it's very helpful to assess your current perspective on life, to consider how your views were formed, and to decide where you need to change.

The accommodating type

If your answers were predominantly "**a**"s and "**b**"s, it suggests that your responses and actions are motivated more by the opinions of others (partner, relatives, friends, the media, society, etc.) than by deeply held convictions of your own. This means that your resolve is less firmly rooted and more likely to falter when effort is required or when circumstances surrounding the issue change. If your main motivation for losing weight is to please your partner, for example, you will be much less likely to stick to a diet than if you want to do it for yourself. If you only recycle trash because your neighbors do, you might stop bothering if you found it inconvenient or tedious.

We are all influenced by those close to us and by the prevailing views of our society—and this can be a positive thing because it keeps us open to the values and opinions of others, and provides the chance to continue learning. Being open-minded to new ideas and influences does not mean that you shouldn't strive to develop your own point of view and inner sense of conviction, however. You will only achieve happiness and fulfillment when you start defining what you yourself really want and consider most important.

The independent type

If your answers were mostly "**c**"s, you are clearly happy to take responsibility for your own personal development. You know where you are heading, both in terms of the person you want to be and the things you want to achieve. Because your goals are inspired by a genuine inner commitment, rather than as a reaction to external pressure, any problems and setbacks you encounter are less likely to knock you off course.

The composite type

If your "**a**"s or "**b**"s are concentrated in some categories but not others, it indicates that you would benefit from focusing on these areas. You might find, for example, that you are clear about what you want to achieve in your career, but are nonetheless quite confused about what your needs are in an intimate relationship.

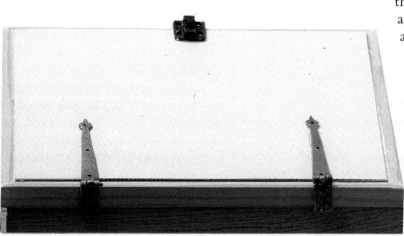

Who Are You?
(pp. 34–35)

Although it's impossible to conclude who you are simply from a short quiz, this self-assessment exercise should provide you with clues about how you see your inner life and the quest to express your individuality. Many people feel guilty about safeguarding the time they need for introspection, but such time is really invaluable. If you find it difficult to make time to be on your own, you can still spend a few hours in serious conversation with intimate friends to explore the richness of your inner life.

Mostly "b"s: Although you recognize the importance of self-knowledge, you frequently find life too demanding to pursue it. There may even be times when you feel you have lost sight of who you are, and wonder if you will ever find yourself again. Attending to your inner life might be one of the things on your never-ending list of things to do, but it is not necessarily your first priority. No matter how fraught things become, however, don't give up. Find the time to read that book, take a meditative walk in the woods, and listen to music and your inner voice. Remember, there are many flowers in your inner garden struggling to bloom.

Mostly "a"s: You are a person who believes that deepening your understanding of yourself is fundamental to building a happy and purposeful life. Everything you do starts with self-analysis, and you probably expect your journey of self-discovery to be a lifelong quest. At your best, you're probably wise and insightful, and may be someone to whom others turn for unobtrusive support and well-considered advice. At your worst, you may be self-absorbed, hesitant, lacking in confidence about your ability to make things happen, and sometimes unrealistic. You may have a closed system of beliefs, and may thus may find it difficult to consider the opinions of others or to heed helpful advice.

Mostly "c"s: Some people find analyzing their feelings disturbing, and you are probably one of them. Emotions can be messy, after all, and concentrating on tangible practicalities makes you feel that you're in control, competent, and able to act like a responsible adult. Another strategy you might employ is filling your life with noise and action to block out thoughts and feelings you don't want to deal with; you may also unconsciously take on the problems of others (and help them get "organized") in order to avoid looking at your own problems. This is unhelpful, because ultimately you will become estranged from your inner self, and, as a consequence, from those close to you.

Have You Got Room to Grow? (pp. 66–67)

Section 1

If you have ticked more statements in this section than any other one, it's likely that you have little self-confidence. Your relationships with people may be based more on a desire for their approval or the need to be liked than on a desire to share or grow. You may feel accepted only when you act as a nice, charming, or attractive person, and may pretend to be intimate and close; in fact, however, you may be close to no-one. Your deepest fear is of rejection because at heart you feel worthless; as a result, you may unconsciously seek out situations or people who criticize you, which only confirms your lack of belief in yourself.

You need to build up your feelings of self-esteem and self-worth, and to begin to be honest and open. Taking the risk to do so will help you enter a new world of deep, enriching relationships.

Section 2

You may give the appearance of someone who is strong, self-sufficient, and independent, and may thus attract weaker, less confident people. In reality, you may often feel lonely, and fear that no-one really understands you. You may have constructed a self-image that doesn't allow you to show any of your weaker, more dependent feelings. Your biggest fear, and perhaps wish, is that someone will see through your facade and perceive who you really are.

You need to think about your fear of being emotionally dependent; perhaps you feel disgusted or ashamed about your needs, which stops you from having deeper relationships. Try experimenting, slowly, with someone you feel you can trust—perhaps telling them something about yourself you've told no-one else. They—and you—may feel greatly relieved to discover you're not superhuman, or as dauntingly capable as you pretend.

Section 3

You both fear and need close relationships. Your dilemma is that being close to someone else feels threatening. You may thus vacillate between being open and being very defensive or aloof with people, which may confuse them.

The need to keep people at arm's length seriously limits your personal growth. However, closeness and independence are not mutually exclusive, and you don't have to sacrifice one in order to have the other. Think hard about why you're frightened of intimacy and solitude. Observe in particular your feelings of wanting to draw back or run away when you're in an intimate situation, and at what point this occurs. What do you fear would happen if you didn't withdraw? If it feels unsafe to let others get close to you, try to discover the reasons why you find it so difficult to trust people.

Feeling ill at ease in your own company suggests that your self-esteem may be low, or that you are anxious about facing your true feelings—so you try to avoid being alone with them. Try going away for a few days of reflection on your own, or set aside at least half-an-hour a day for quiet solitude. You may discover that you're not as fearful as you think you are, and that introspection is restorative.

Section 4

Our earliest relationships are a blueprint for all future relationships. If your family life was marred by tension and anger, you may grow up believing that this is how people relate to one another, or that to show your softer side makes you vulnerable to pain and humiliation. Similarly, if the atmosphere was polite but repressed, you may believe that real feelings are threatening, and that keeping up the appearance of civility is all that matters.

Take time to think about which parent you think you're most like, and why. This is the person with whom you most identified as a child, and on whom you're probably modeling your adult behavior. Reflect, too, on how your parents' behavior and your relationship with your brothers and sisters have determined your attitude to others and yourself. If you felt you constantly had to compete with your siblings for attention, you may be equally competitive with your peers and colleagues, which might make them uncomfortable.

What's Stopping You?
(pp. 88-89)

Add up how many "**a**"s, "**b**"s, "**c**"s, and "**d**"s you've ticked, then read the relevant comments below.

Mostly "a"s

Although you may get more things done than other people, you seem to have a compulsive need to plan, probably as a way of making you feel safe and in control of your life. You may be compensating for a fear of "going with the flow" to the extent that you're not open to new ideas or change, or perhaps suffer from an exaggerated fear of failure. When did you last do something on the spur of the moment or on a whim? You need to loosen your grip on life and understand why the thought of losing control makes you feel so anxious.

Mostly "b"s

You probably can feel quite confident in some situations; you will carefully assess your options, coming up with effective strategies and moving ahead when you feel safe, but will then pull back and suddenly become indecisive or anxious if you feel unsafe. Consider in which areas of your life you tend to procrastinate or panic unnecessarily. You can then think about what it is that you find frightening, or what makes you feel nervous—and strive to develop greater confidence in yourself.

Mostly "c"s

You may find it difficult to commit yourself to anything unless you feel absolutely sure it will succeed. This can enormously restrict your potential to grow. Think about which situations make you feel particularly inhibited; you may discover, for example, that it's in the area of work or relationships that you back off or withdraw. You can then work out ways to change.

Mostly "d"s

You may be locked into a way of thinking and behaving that doesn't allow you to change or move in any direction without creating intense anxiety and indecision. Perhaps you feel it's better to stay still and not rock the boat. You may feel safe, but are probably spending a lot of time and energy maintaining a false sense of security and cultivating a defensive, "who cares?" attitude. You may also feel frustrated, but are unwilling to recognize how stuck you are. You need to get to grips with the deeper reasons for your anxiety about change, and to find ways to overcome your fears.

INDEX

BIBLIOGRAPHY

Richard Nelson Bolles, *What Color Is Your Parachute?*; Ten Speed Press, California, U.S., (updated annually)

Deepak Chopra, *Creating Health*; Grafton Books, London, U.K., 1987

Stephen R. Covey, *The 7 Habits of Highly Effective People*; Fireside, New York, NY, U.S., 1990

Stephanie Dowrick, *Intimacy & Solitude Self-Therapy Book*; The Women's Press, London, U.K., 1993

Windy Dryden, *10 Steps to Positive Living*; Sheldon Press, London, U.K., 1994

Louise L. Hay, *The Power Is Within You*; Eden Grove Editions, London, U.K., 1991

Lynda Field, *Creating Self-Esteem*; Element Books Limited, Shaftesbury, Dorset, U.K., 1993

Liz Hodgkinson, *Personal Growth Handbook*; Judy Piatkus (Publishers) Ltd., London, U.K., 1993

Susan Jeffers, *Feel the Fear and Do It Anyway*; Arrow Books Limited, London, U.K., 1991

Sarah Litvinoff, *The Relate Guide to Better Relationships*; Ebury Press, London, U.K., 1991

Ursula Markham, *Life Scripts: How to Talk to Yourself for Positive Results*; Element Books Limited, Shaftesbury, Dorset, U.K., 1993

Ursula Markham, *Your Four-Point Plan for Life*; Element Books Limited, Shaftesbury, Dorset, U.K., 1991

Vera Peiffer, *Positively Fearless*; Element Books Limited, Shaftesbury, Dorset, U.K., 1993

Vera Peiffer, *Strategies of Optimism*; Element Books Limited, Shaftesbury, Dorset, U.K., 1990

William J. Reilly, *How to Get What You Want Out of Life*; HarperCollins, London, U.K., 1987

Dorothy Rowe, *The Successful Self*; HarperCollins, London, U.K., 1989

Dorothy Rowe, *Wanting Everything*; HarperCollins, London, U.K., 1991

Gail Sheehy, *Passages: Predictable Crises of Adult Life*; E.P. Dutton, New York, NY, U.S., 1974

Robin Skynner and John Cleese, *Life and How to Survive It*; Methuen, London, U.K., 1993

Stafford Whiteaker, *The Good Retreat Guide*; Rider, London, U.K., 1991

CREDITS

Illustrators
Gillian Best, Steve Cummiskey, Roy Flooks, Anthony Limerick, Romy O'Driscoll, Emma Parker/Private View (agent), Martin Ridgewell, Colin Williams

Children's drawings on p. 28: Charlotte Gruen, Sadiq Mansur

Modelmakers
Gail Armstrong, Atlas Models, Mark Jamieson, James Mackinnon, Jeremy Pegg, Mike Shepherd, Justin Wilson

Photographers
Maria Beddoes, Jonathan Byles, Mark Gaskin, David Glick, Mark Hamilton, Sheena Land, Neil Phillips, Mark Preston, Jonny Thompson, Alex Wilson

Picture sources
The publishers are grateful to the following individuals and picture libraries for permission to reproduce their photographs:

The Garden Picture Library *Ron Sutherland* 120; **The Image Bank** *Ross M. Horowitz* 106-107; **Images Colour Library** 62, 112, 136-137; **Sporting Pictures (U.K.) Ltd.** 124; **Tony Stone** *Steve Taylor* 14, 32, 86; *John Warden* 44-45; **Telegraph Colour Library** *Jean Louis Batt* 21 (top); **Zefa Pictures Ltd.** 69